To order additional copies of
Do It Right!
Love, Sex, and Relationships God's Way
by D. C. Edmond,
call 1-800-765-6955.

Visit us at *www.reviewandherald.com*
for information on other Review and Herald products.

D. C. EDMOND

Do It Right!

Love, Sex, and Relationships God's Way

REVIEW AND HERALD® PUBLISHING ASSOCIATION
HAGERSTOWN, MD 21740

The author assumes full responsibility for the accuracy of all facts and quotations as cited in this book.

Unless otherwise noted, Bible texts in this book are from the *Holy Bible, New International Version.* Copyright © 1973, 1978, 1984, International Bible Society. Used by permission of Zondervan Bible Publishers.

This book was
Edited by Lori Peckham
Designed by Trent Truman
Photographs by Joel D. Springer/Digitally modified
Electronic makeup by Shirley M. Bolivar
Typeset: 11/13 Usherwood

PRINTED IN U.S.A.

04 03 02 01   5 4 3 2 1

R&H Cataloging Service
Edmond, D. C.
    Do it right! love, sex, and relationships God's way.

    1. Sexual abstinence   2. Chastity   3. Dating (social customs).
I. Title

306.73

ISBN 0-8280-1445-0

Dedication

TO MY WIFE, JILL.
Of all the people who were vital
to the writing of this book,
no one was, or is, more vital than she.

Acknowledgments

I have so many people to thank, but (my editors tell me) so little space! So, here goes:

First, to the people at the Review and Herald Publishing Association. Thanks for the opportunity you've given me. I grew up reading books published by the Review and Herald, starting with Uncle Arthur books, which I read about a thousand times each. Little did I dream, while reading Review and Herald books on Friday nights and Sabbath afternoons, that one day they'd publish one of mine.

Second, to Lori Peckham, Michelle Sturm, Andrea Tymeson, and Kelli Gauthier at *Insight* magazine. There would absolutely be no book without them. Their encouragement and patience have made working with *Insight* a joy.

Thanks also to the secretarial staff of the Office of Youth Ministries at the South Central Conference—in particular, Mrs. Alicia Ford Hunt and Ms. Kanika M. McIntyre. They are great—and that's understating it.

Finally, thanks to my family. To my mother, Mrs. Marcelle Edmond, for instilling in me a love of books. To my dad, Elder J. H. Edmond, for working so hard to give my two sisters, my brother, and me a Christian education so that we could read the books that both my mom and my dad taught us to love. (Sadly, right after I finished this book, I lost my dad, suddenly and unexpectedly, to cancer. It saddens me, more than I can ever say, that my dad will never see this book. But it makes me so happy that God has promised that if I am faithful, I'll see my dad again. I want that more than anything.)

Thanks also to my children, Courtney, now 18, and R.J., now 14. Thanks for providing the material for my column in *Insight* and for being good sports and allowing me to use it—at least allowing me to use *most* of it.

It would take a whole book to thank my wife, Mrs. Jill R. Edmond. Suffice it to say that I couldn't have done anything I've done these past 22 years without her. Nor would I have wanted to.

Contents

Preface

i was working in my office in the South Central Conference when the phone rang, an event that happens scores of times each day. On the other end was Lori Peckham, editor of *Insight*, asking me to write a column on "love and relationships" for *Insight* magazine.

About a year later the phone rang again. It was Jeannette Johnson, the acquisitions editor for the Review and Herald Publishing Association, asking me if the Review and Herald could publish a book of my articles. I couldn't believe it—I still can't! But if you're reading this, I guess it must be true. (Even if you're *not* reading this—because, after all, how many people really read the preface?—I guess it's true anyway!)

Over the past two years I've met via mail young people from Canada to Africa as they've sent questions to my column. Some of the questions made me laugh, some made me sad, others scared the daylights out of me. (My very first question was from a young lady who was secretly going with her foster brother—who *also* lived in the house with her *and* who was into drugs. That scared *me*, and probably everyone else who has a teenage daughter [or a teenage foster son]!)

As I've traveled I've also had people come up to me and say, "Aren't you the guy who writes that column for *Insight?*" It's been a wonderful privilege being affiliated with *Insight*. And I've enjoyed the opportunities I've gotten from that affiliation, including writing this book.

Thanks for all the questions. Please, keep on sending them. And keep on reading *Insight!*

Dating 101

"WHY ARE GUYS SO STRANGE?"

I've liked this guy all my life, and for a while I thought he liked me back. Then two years ago my brothers started teasing him about hanging out with me, so he stopped.

Now he's dating this other girl who asked him out (and who *used to* talk about how unattractive he is!). He says he hates her, but they're still dating.

I'm so confused. I've liked him forever, and he knows it. I'm trying to be his friend, but I get mad at him and his girlfriend.

How come life is *so* unfair? And how come guys are *so* strange?

As the father of a teenage daughter, I agree—guys *are* strange. I try to tell my daughter this all the time, but she won't listen! (Sorry, guys; I really don't dislike you. It's just that I'll like you a whole lot better when my daughter is finished with grad school and has started her career. Once she finishes school, I'll be *delighted* for her to find a nice Seventh-day Adventist young man—*with a job*—so she can start spending *his* money instead of *mine*.)

Anyway, sometimes the only thing worse than *not* getting what we want is actually to *get* it. You really want this guy, right?

But let's look at this. He *knows* you like him, yet he's dating someone else (whom he says he hates). Now, there's a loyal boyfriend for you! And he stopped hanging around you because your brothers teased him.

Are you sure you really *want* this relationship? He's probably a nice fellow, but you might want to look more critically at the characteristics he's displayed in his relationships—disloyalty (he hates his girlfriend but keeps on dating her) and wimpiness (he stopped hanging around you because your brothers teased him). Is this what you really want?

You probably still want him, and I understand. I liked a girl from the time I was 6 years old until I was about 20, and she knew it. She kind of strung me along all those years—because I was *willing* to be strung along.

If that's what you want, I understand; I was there. But I'd rather see you be *nice* to this young fellow (which doesn't mean be around him all the time, because it's hard to get over a person that way) but be *gone*.

"I DON'T UNDERSTAND GIRLS"

Why are girls so hard to understand?

If I had an easy answer to that question, I think people would pay me big bucks for it!

I've been married for more than 20 years to a wonderful person, but even after all this time I confess that I still don't always understand my wife.

Take Christmas shopping, for example. My wife likes

to drop hints, and my children and I are supposed to figure out what she really wants.

I don't understand that. Suppose I *miss* the hint, which I frequently do (I'm not very good at catching hints).

But my wife wants to be *surprised* at Christmas. I don't understand that, either.

When my sister-in-law called me this past Christmas and asked me what I wanted, I told her the title of a book, the author, and where she could buy it. I'd rather *expect* a gift and get what I *want* than be *surprised* and get something I *don't* want.

Not my wife. She wants me to put some thought into it.

Well, when I do think about it, I think about the fact that I don't have money to waste. So if she'd just *tell* me what she wants, I'd buy it, and we'd *both* be happy. But she wants to be surprised, to which *I* say, "Bah, humbug!"

Anyway, we tend not to understand people who aren't like us. Women are different from men physically (but you knew that already!), and I suspect they're different in other ways as well.

Some feminists will tell you that there aren't any differences between men and women other than the physical ones. Well, I don't agree, though even the physical differences tend to make understanding each other a challenge.

Take, for example, the fact that women can bear children, and we men (praise the Lord!) can't. Since there's pain involved in childbirth, I don't understand why a woman would want to go through it a second or third time (and in some cases a fourth, fifth, sixth, etc., time). I believe in *avoiding* pain.

"Why?" I used to ask my wife when we'd debate whether or not to have a second child. "Why do you want to go through all that *again?*"

I still don't know why she wanted to—but I'm glad she did. Otherwise, I wouldn't have my son. (I suspect there would be fewer children in the world if men had to bear them!)

You know, I'm glad that my wife and I *are* different (at least *most* of the time). I wouldn't want my wife to be just like me. I've learned so much and my life has been so enriched by the diversity in our home, which includes my daughter (who's more like me) and my son (who's more like my wife).

I just wish my wife would come right out and tell me what she wants for Christmas!

"WHY IS DATING SO CONFUSING?"

Why does dating sometimes leave me confused and in despair?

That's exactly what I've been trying to tell my teenage daughter—that dating will leave her confused and in despair! However, I tell her that once she's finished grad school, gets a good job, moves out of Daddy's house, and stops spending Daddy's money, *then* dating (Seventh-day Adventist Christian guys) will be a *wonderful* thing.

Of course, she hasn't bought into my philosophy yet—at least not the part about not dating until after grad school. But I'll keep trying!

Now, about dating: I really believe that in order for any relationship to work, the people involved have to open up and be emotionally vulnerable. When you do that, you're saying to the other person, "Here I am. I'm letting you see me as I am. I'm not hiding even my bad points, because I'm trusting you to accept me the way I am."

Well, that works as long as the relationship works. And while things are good, it's wonderful to have someone to share things with.

But what happens when that person we've opened up to and shared our lives with doesn't want to be a part of our lives anymore?

I'll tell you what happens: confusion (How could someone who did want me suddenly *not* want me?), despair (What's wrong with me?), etc.

This is as much a part of the dating scenario as the excitement and good times. It's the other part of the dating game, and about the only way to avoid it is to stay out of the game.

Even though I'd rather not be the one to tell you this, please listen to me. If you're a teenager and you're involved in a relationship right now, chances are that you *won't* be in one soon—at least not with the same person.

That's right. Even if you and your boyfriend/girlfriend are flying high now, chances are that you will, fairly soon, "crash and burn." And part of the pain of the "crash landing" comes from its unexpectedness—because you thought what the two of you had would last forever.

Hello? It probably won't. That's the bad news.

The good news is that, first, the pain won't last forever. And second, the Lord will get you through the pain, hurt, confusion, and despair—this time and the next time too.

Yes, there will be a next time. I don't want to paint too gloomy a picture of relationships (unless you're my daughter!). But life on this earth is never pain-free. Don't look for heaven in the things of this earth—especially not in teenage romance.

But just as surely as there are tears and pain in this life, there is a God who wipes away tears and eases pain.

"SHOULD WE DATE ONLY TO PREPARE FOR MARRIAGE?"

Do you believe that dating means preparing for marriage?

If your question means what I think it does—that every person you date should be viewed as a potential marriage partner down the road (*way* down the road in the case of most of you who read *Insight*)—then my answer is yes. Here's why I believe that.

From a practical perspective, you never know how things will end up once you start going out with a person.

I remember how I got with my wife, Jill. My intent—can I be honest?—was *not* to become involved with the future Mrs. Edmond!

I was *really* interested in one of Jill's friends. But I thought that Jill wouldn't approve of my relationship with her friend. (You ladies know how you are. If you disapprove of your friend's boyfriend, he has a tough time getting his foot in the door.)

So I figured that if I picked the person most likely to oppose me—Jill—and won her over to my side, then when I was ready to make my move toward this other young lady, I'd have an ally.

Well, it worked, but not the way I expected. I did such a great job of winning over Jill that I not only gained an ally—I gained a *wife!*

Like I said, you never know where things will lead. And since you never know how things will *end,* it's better that some things just don't *start.*

With that in mind, I think young people should have standards for the people they date. You ought not to date just anybody. If the person you want to date is unsuitable to marry and you *know* that, then what are you accomplishing by going out with them?

Too many people end up in unhappy marriages because they married someone unsuitable, someone who didn't meet their standards—just so they could be "with" *somebody*. And it's almost impossible to *marry* someone unsuitable unless you *date* someone unsuitable.

Now, when I say "unsuitable," I'm not talking about being a snob and/or looking down on people. And I'm not talking about thinking you're better than someone.

I'm talking about the *character* of the people you date—how they are when it's just the two of you. I'm also talking about their principles and values.

Any person you choose to—as the old folk used to say—"keep company with" ought to have character, principles, and values. And if they *don't,* why are you with them?

"HOW SHOULD A HEALTHY RELATIONSHIP PROGRESS?"

How should a healthy relationship progress? I'm 17, so I know I'm not getting married soon, but I don't want the relationship to go backwards, either.

That's a good question, and it shows that you're looking at your relationship from a realistic angle. You know you're not getting married soon, because you're only 17. That's realistic. (Though some people do get married that young, I can't see any situation in which that would be a good idea.)

Even if you are fully emotionally mature at 17 (and I don't know many people who are), how many of you have jobs that make it possible to support yourselves?

Let's say you make as much as $7 per hour, which, at 17, most of you probably *don't* make. That means at 40 hours per week your gross pay is $280 a week, or $1,120 a month.

Let's subtract roughly 30 percent off the top of that for tithe and taxes. That leaves you about $780. The single ladies in my office tell me a one-bedroom apartment here in Nashville is between $450 and $500 a month (and the cost of living here is fairly low compared to the East or West Coast).

That puts you at $330 (unless you get a roommate—good luck with that!). After you get a decent used car and pay insurance, you're down to about $20 a month, or $5 a week, and you haven't even eaten yet. I've seen some of you eat, and $5 per *meal* isn't enough, much less $5 per week! And don't forget other expenses such as clothes, gas, and entertainment.

So you're right, getting married at 17 isn't realistic. But let's talk about: ". . . I don't want the relationship to go backwards." Sounds good, but what does it mean? When you're 17, how far "forward" can a relationship realistically go?

The reality is that all romantic male-female relationships between two people who aren't married will come to an end of some kind. They will end in either marriage or a breakup. These are the only two places a healthy relationship can go. The average dating relationship will take off, level off, then break off, until the Lord leads you to the person with whom you will share your life.

So my advice is this: treat the person with whom you are involved the way you wish to be treated, and enjoy the relationship for what it is—at 17, probably a learning experience and a stepping-stone.

"HOW DO YOU KNOW YOU'VE FOUND THE RIGHT ONE?"

How do you know whether the person you're dating is the "right one"?

If I had an easy answer to that question, *Insight*—and everyone else—would probably have to pay me a whole lot of money!

I do believe, however, that there are some clues that can help you figure out if, as Ray Charles put it in the old soft drink commercial, "you've got the right one, baby."

First of all, does the Word of God say your relationship is OK? For instance, if you're involved in an "unequally yoked" relationship that 2 Corinthians 6:14 talks about, then that person isn't Mr. or Ms. Right. If your relationship goes against *anything* He commands in the Bible, then you know that person isn't right for you.

Remember, just as God brings people together, so does the devil. And right now there are a bunch of people in relationships in which the devil has served as the matchmaker. That's kind of scary to me!

Besides making sure your relationship is in harmony with God, you have to make sure that Mr. or Ms. Right has come into your life at the *right* time. I mean, if you're 16 and you've found Mr./Ms. Right, what can you really do about it? You can date him/her for a while, but the odds of your relationship lasting permanently are pretty slim—unless you get married early.

And that's usually not a good idea. Why? One reason is that most of you are going to have a hard time funding an education at an Adventist college. It'll cost you between $60,000 and $100,000, even with your parents' financial support. And it's much harder to go to school if you're

21

newly married, just starting a home, and not making much more than minimum wage.

Even if you found a job paying $10 per hour and could fit in 40 hours a week of work *plus* go to school *and* study, when would you have any time to spend with your new husband or wife?

At $10 an hour you'd make a little less than $21,000 a year. Subtract 20 percent for taxes, another 15 percent for tithes and offerings, and now you're down to about $13,000. That's less than your tuition costs.

But you say, "Oh, my husband/wife will work too." Well, OK, but doesn't your spouse want to go to college too? Even if he/she found a job paying $10 an hour, worked 40 hours a week, and studied (now the two of you *really* won't see each other!), you're looking at a $28,000-$40,000 tuition bill. And the two of you make only $42,000!

So if you find Mr./Ms. Right, the time has to be right. And during high school or academy usually isn't the right time for a permanent relationship. You might find someone who's right for that time, but it's only temporary.

Now, contrary to what some people think, the most important way to tell if you're dating Mr./Ms. Right is *not* by the way you *feel.* Feelings are not a safe guide at all.

I've never forgotten the time a man in the church I was pastoring got involved with a young lady who was not his wife. He looked me straight in the eye and said, "I believe God is going to be glorified in this relationship" (meaning his adulterous relationship).

But by what God says in the Ten Commandments, I *know* that He isn't glorified in an adulterous relationship! We can tell ourselves anything we want to. But it's what God tells us in His Word that counts.

Let me share one last factor to keep in mind when considering whether or not you've found Mr./Ms. Right: *The right person will help you live the right way.*

If God is really in your relationship, then being with this person will make you a better person. But if being with this person affects your spiritual life negatively—you pray less, study God's Word less, and come to His house less—then I think "you've got the wrong one, baby!"

If the person you're with isn't helping you become a better Christian, then you need to tell him or her goodbye.

Before the Breath Mints

"WHY CAN'T I GET A DATE?"

Why can't I get a date? Do guys think I'm ugly or something?

i don't know what the guys think, but I think it's difficult to be a Seventh-day Adventist female once you're past the age of about 11. Of all the places I've visited in all the years I've been in this church (which is all my life), I have seldom been in a place where Adventist males outnumbered Adventist females.

That means that somebody is always going to get left out of the dating game, including some attractive people. In fact, I've known some ladies who didn't get asked out because they *were* attractive.

I knew a lady like that when I was a student at Oakwood College back in (as my children would say) "the old days." She asked that same question. She was very attractive, but never got asked out because all the guys (including me!) were too scared to ask her. We all thought she'd say no, so no one ever asked.

One of the great myths out there in "femaleland" is

that guys do not mind getting rejected when they ask a young lady out on a date. Think again. Nobody likes rejection, including guys, some of whom will go to great lengths to avoid it.

If you're a young lady and you've never asked a guy out, it's possible that you don't know how difficult it can be. Even though it was "100 years ago," I still remember how nervous I got.

The young lady would never know, however, because I never showed it. But inside I was dying! I became very good at manufacturing ways of being around the young ladies I wanted to be around without actually asking them out.

Ladies, ever notice the guy who is *always* hanging around you at your banquets, basketball games, etc.? It is possible that he wants to ask you out, but he's afraid you'll say no. So he hangs around all the time, thus gaining your company without risking your *rejection.*

It's a good trick. I know. I used it all the time.

There were some risks attached to that strategy, though. Sometimes guys with more nerve would ask out the young ladies I was hanging around. But my strategy worked more often than it didn't. The point is, not having a date may not be your fault.

But suppose guys really are avoiding you. What can you do? Well, it's almost against the "code of fathers with teenage daughters" for me to tell you teenage girls how to increase your chances of getting dates. But I've got to answer this question honestly (and then go home and hide this book from my daughter!).

First, ask yourself: Am I approachable? Am I friendly and nice to everyone—not just to get a date, but because I'm treating people the way Jesus would treat them?

I knew a lady when I was at Oakwood College who acted as if she were God's gift to men. Most of the men decided that God was going to have to find her someone to date, because *they* weren't going to date her. Thinking that you're "all that" is bad news for your dating life.

Second, ask yourself: Am I presentable? You don't have to wear designer clothes every day, but looking as though you are auditioning for the part of the scarecrow on the *Wizard of Oz* isn't going to help your dating life.

A nice personality and a neat appearance go a long way. Let's be honest—how many really *great*-looking people do you know? Most people seem attractive based on more than just how they look.

Last (and I *really* don't want my daughter to see this— maybe the editors can print this part in Spanish!), if the occasion presents itself, *you* do the asking. Most academies and institutions have functions and reverse weekends during which the ladies get to do the asking. Use these occasions.

"I DON'T WANT HIM TO KNOW I LIKE HIM"

How can I just be friends with guys I like without them knowing I really like them?

I know ladies have been taught since creation "not to let a guy know that they like him." I don't want to go against what you ladies have been taught, but I just don't understand that kind of thinking.

You like a guy, but you don't want him to think that you like him? What do you want him to think—that you *don't* like him? And if you succeed in making him think that you're not interested in him (even if you *are),* then why should he approach you to ask you out?

I've never understood this tactic, and you know what? I don't think you ladies can explain it either. You tell all your friends that you like Mr. X, but you want Mr. X to think that you want to be "just friends."

Now, I'm not advocating chasing young fellows all over the place and throwing yourself at them, but this isn't the Victorian era. The days of playing these guess-how-I-feel-about-you games are almost gone.

There are ways you can let fellows know you're interested in them. Most schools have a Sadie Hawkins-type event in which the young women ask out the young men. Take advantage of that opportunity, ladies!

At a school I visited once, all the young ladies were complaining that the fellows were immature because they seemed reluctant to ask them to the big upcoming school event. I asked the ladies if there were any times they were supposed to ask the fellows to an event. They said "Yes," but then confessed that they didn't do it.

If you ladies are interested in a young fellow but try not to show it, you confuse the poor fellow. Everybody isn't like me, but back in the Dark Ages, when I was young, I didn't want to be confused about how someone felt. That's why I always skipped over the "game players."

Maybe I'm just old and slow, but I don't get it. Why do you want the people you like to think you don't like them?

"WHAT'S THE BEST WAY TO APPROACH A GIRL?"

I'm a 15-year-old guy, and I'd like to know how I'm supposed to walk up to a girl and tell her I like her. What's the best way to approach a girl and start a conversation with her while keeping all this as Christian as possible?

i assume you're talking about a girl you don't already know. And I'm not sure there *is* a way to approach someone you've never met before and say, "Hello, I'm Joe, and I just want to tell you that I like you."

If you've never met the girl, how do you know you like her? Almost all you know about her is how she looks. Ever been out with someone who didn't look bad, but had *no* personality? Or someone who couldn't carry on an intelligent conversation? I have—back in my young days. It was no fun.

But what you probably mean is "How do you approach someone you think you might like to get to know?"

First, let me tell you what is almost certainly *not* a good approach—to go up to a young lady and pull out some weak line you saw some actor use on TV. Remember that the lady to whom the actor was saying that "line" is called an *actress*. Which means that if she responds positively to the "line," it's because she's being paid to. Besides, I'm not sure that anyone who falls for "Yo, baby—what's up?" is someone you really want to date.

Based on conversations I've had with young ladies, the best approach seems to be a simple introduction followed by an attempt to start up a conversation. Questions such as "Where are you from?" can help you establish some things you might have in common.

You want to establish some common ground so you'll have something to talk about. That's all you can really do at first, anyway—talk. The problem is that young people see someone and decide they'd like to establish some kind of *relationship*. Relationships take time and work.

The young ladies I talked to also said that it's important to be yourself. Even in the unlikely event that the smooth line from TV works for you, what are you going to do next? Run home and watch more TV to learn some more smooth lines?

If the lines you've gotten from somebody ever work, then you'll always have to be that somebody. Wouldn't it just be easier to be yourself?

"THERE'S THIS SHY GUY"

I like this guy at church who's two years older than I am. I've known him all my life, but I'm afraid to approach him. He seems shy. What should I do?

Since I received this anonymous question via e-mail, I'm going to give you an answer based on these three assumptions: (1) you're old enough to date, (2) your parents approve of this young fellow, and (3) you're a young lady. Now, if any of my assumptions are wrong (but I don't think they are), we've got some other problems.

I'm thinking that my answer may be another one that sparks letters of disagreement, but anyway, here goes.

I've *never* seen anything wrong with a young lady indicating her interest in a young man before he "makes the first move." (*Unless* that young lady is my daughter! Now, I have to say I'm only kidding, because my daughter will read this book.)

I'm not talking about a girl acting boy-crazy and chasing some guy all over creation. But you tell me, *Where is it written that the guy always has to make the first move and the girl does* nothing, ever, *until he does?*

Personally, I think you ladies hide behind that "It's-not-ladylike-to-make-the-first-move" myth because it feels safe. Well, think about it: if you sit back and do nothing, you never get rejected.

Now, I understand that you don't like rejection. But whoever told you that *guys* do? Please.

Let's get real. If the guy you're talking about is shy, if

he's afraid to make the first move, and if *you* don't want to make it either, how do the two of you get anywhere? And please don't give me that tired "Well-if-he-doesn't-make-the-first-move-it's-not-meant-to-be" line. That's an excuse.

There are dignified ways for you ladies to let a guy know you're interested in him. That was true even back in the Dark Ages, when I was in academy and college. Some women were doing that then, and some are doing that now.

Of course, *I've* never tried to get a guy to like *me*. So I asked my single 22-year-old secretary, Ms. Kanika McIntyre, for her ideas. She suggests: (1) if the guy is into basketball or sports, go to the major events he participates in; (2) compliment him on his positive achievements; (3) make conversation with him. Those good ideas will get you started.

The truth is, if you don't figure out a way to let Brother Shy Guy know you're interested in him—and if he's worth having as a boyfriend—some other young lady *will*.

"HOW DO I GET SOMEONE TO LIKE ME?"

How do I get a guy to like me?

Well, I don't have any experience getting *guys* to like me. But I *am* a guy (an old guy by teenage standards), so I'll share what worked for me.

First of all, I'm not sure you can *get* someone to like someone. If whatever it is that draws people to each other isn't there, I'm not sure there's any way to put it there.

But sometimes it's not that the person you're interested in isn't interested in you—he may not have noticed you. You may just need to get his attention.

Now, there are several ways to do that. Remember, though, that there's a difference between negative attention and positive attention.

An example of negative attention happened a while ago in a church where I preached. Just before I started the sermon, a young lady came walking down the aisle *very* slowly, in a *very* short skirt. She sat down in the front row. The church was large, and it took this girl a long time to make her way down front. She certainly got everyone's attention!

That's negative attention—you don't want that kind of attention. On the other hand, if a young fellow is going to like you, he *does* need to know you're alive.

Back in the Dark Ages—when I was young—I always figured that if I could spend enough time with the person in whom I was interested, I had a chance. To make sure she knew I was alive, I would arrange it so I ended up somewhere she was.

One way I spent time with certain young ladies was to make sure I came in just behind them in the cafeteria line. Often the cafeteria would be crowded, and then we would *have* to eat together. That put my "foot in the door."

Figure out some way to get your foot in the door. But remember, you are a valuable person with something positive to bring to a Christian relationship. You don't need to throw yourself at anybody!

"SHOULD I ASK HER OUT?"

There's this girl I really like, and she likes me, too. Actually, I don't just *like* her—I've had this huge crush on her for more than a year. But I can't get the courage to ask her out. What should I do? Should I ask her out?

The short answer to that question is yes, if:
1. You and she are old enough to date.
2. You are both Seventh-day Adventists.

3. Both your parents and hers approve.

4. This young lady isn't my daughter. (Don't take that personally! I don't want anyone asking my daughter out until she's 25 and finished with grad school. My daughter doesn't agree with me, though!)

I also recommend that when you get up the courage to ask this young lady for a date, make it a group date. I don't see the need for teenagers to be doing a lot of single dating.

This is a good opportunity for me to point out to the ladies how difficult it is for many fellows to get up the nerve to ask you for a date. I've had young ladies tell me that it's not hard for guys to ask girls out. If a girl says no, it doesn't bother the guy because:

1. He usually doesn't act like it bothers him. (Do you *expect* him to break down and cry in front of you? Of course he's going to *act* like it doesn't bother him—but it does. Nobody likes rejection!)

2. It's the guy's lot in life to ask, and the girl's lot in life to say yes or no. And guys have to accept the risk of being turned down as a part of life.

That's nonsense. Ladies, think of the few times you've asked guys out. If they said no (particularly if they did it insensitively), do you mean to tell me that it didn't bother you? Of course it did. It bothers guys, too.

For some guys just the possibility that they might be turned down paralyzes them with fear. I know—100 years ago I was one of those guys.

For the past 20 years the Lord has given me some wonderful opportunities to preach in many different places for up to 4,000 people at a time. But never in my life have I been as nervous as I got when I asked ladies out on dates. They never knew it, but I was terrified.

I was so terrified, in fact, that I never asked out some ladies. Sometimes guys with more courage than I asked those young ladies, and in some cases they wound up marrying them. So, fellows, you can watch and admire a young lady from afar, but one day you'll "watch" her go down the aisle with someone else!

Ladies, be sensitive. When a fellow asks you out, during that instant you hold his feelings in your hands (no matter how hard he's trying to hide that fact). Handle those feelings with care. Remember, what goes around comes around.

"WHERE SHOULD WE GO ON A DATE?"

Where are some nice clean places for teens to go on dates?

A good place for teenagers to go on dates is anywhere there are lots of lights and chaperons!

Now that we've covered that, let me point out that the answer depends on your taste. For example, I'm a sports person. I would enjoy sports-related dates such as going to a ball game (especially to see the Cleveland Indians play!), skating, or playing miniature golf with about eight or 10 *other people* in a *group* setting. Get the hint?

Maybe you're more musically inclined. There are some nice groups that you, your date, and *your other friends* might enjoy hearing in concert. (I'm not talking about some obscenity-spewing rap group or some eardrum-shattering rock group.)

If you are blessed enough to be attending an Adventist academy (and I know that not all of you consider yourselves blessed, but you are), take advantage of the events the school offers. First of all, school events usually cost less (when they cost at all). Plus, your parents are far more likely to agree to let you go out with your boyfriend/girlfriend if you're going to a school function or even a church activity.

There was no way I would let my daughter go on a date to an amusement park when she was a freshman in academy. But when our church went there, I let her go, knowing that she and her girlfriends would spend the day with their male "friends." I even gave her extra spending money. What was I thinking?

Building dates around meals has been popular for years but has its risks. One time I noticed that one of my friends and her boyfriend were putting on some weight. She explained that the main reason was because *all* their dates consisted of going out to eat. They got bigger, but they had fun.

Dating is a time for good clean fun. You don't have to spend a lot of money, do anything elaborate, or (surprise!) have your hands all over each other to have fun.

And don't fall for the "I don't know what we're going to do; let's just go for a ride" trick, ladies. The fellows who take you on those kinds of dates only *sound* like they have nothing planned. Believe me, they have a plan!

If you and your date *and a group* of other young people enjoy being around each other, almost anything you plan will be a good date.

Timing Is Everything

"AT WHAT AGE SHOULD WE BE ALLOWED TO DATE?"

At what age should teens be allowed to date?

Well, 25 works for me (smile)!

The reality is that if you are in academy (which some of you are), then there are opportunities provided for you to "date" in a group setting beginning about ninth grade, or age 14. Many of you in other settings have opportunities to group-date around that same age.

Group dating gives you the opportunity to get to know members of the opposite sex in a relatively safe environment, without the temptation that often accompanies dates where there are only two people.

I know what your next question is: "At what age should teens be able to *single*-date [go on a date alone, without supervision]?"

Well, 35 works for me (smile)!

Seriously, think for a minute about the enormous pressure that goes into single dating. Here are two young people. In all likelihood there's at least some physical attraction between them (in some cases there is a *major* physical attraction).

Single dating is going to put those two young people in a setting in which they are alone for at least part of their date. Now, you tell me—doesn't the idea of leaving alone two young people who may have a strong physical attraction sound potentially dangerous, at least a little?

Right about now all of you are screaming, "But we're not going to do anything!"

You're right. Not everyone will. But enough young people do make compromises and wrong choices.

I was at a rap session with a large group of teenagers a year or so ago, and I asked the group: "How many of you have done things on a date that you knew you shouldn't have done and have regretted doing?" Virtually every hand went up.

I am not going to tell you never to single-date. You wouldn't listen if I did. I *am* saying that a lot of people can't handle it without making some kind of compromise.

"MY FRIENDS ARE PRESSURING ME TO DATE"

I'm 16, and I feel like I'm too young to date. But some of my friends keep pressuring me to get involved with this guy who is 18. Should I compromise my beliefs and get involved with this guy who wants to date me, or should I hold on to my beliefs?

If you've been reading my column in *Insight* regularly, you've probably heard my principles relative to relationships and dating. Here they are again:

○ Wait until you're 25 and finished with graduate

school before you begin dating or even *thinking* about the opposite sex. (OK, that's not really a rule, just wishful thinking for all of us fathers with teenage daughters.)

○ Don't share your life with anyone who doesn't share your values.

○ Always treat your boyfriend/girlfriend the way you wish to be treated.

○ If you can't tell your parents about a relationship, you shouldn't have one.

○ Always listen to your parents when they're talking to you about teenage romance—especially your father, ladies. (OK, that's not a real rule either, but I tried to stick it in.)

○ Here's another really important rule: *Never compromise your beliefs and principles for the sake of a relationship.* I can't think of a scenario in which sticking to this rule didn't turn out to be a good idea.

If you think you're too young to date at 16 (that sound you hear in the background is just other parents shouting "amen" and "hallelujah" at the idea of a 16-year-old deciding she's too young to date), then don't be pressured by your friends into a relationship. Your friends aren't the ones who have to deal with the relationship—you do. So you make the decision.

Once you get on the "I-am-doing-this-because-of-my-friends" train—for any reason—it's hard to get off. And usually that train is going nowhere.

"HOW CAN I TALK MY DAD INTO LETTING ME DATE?"

How can I talk my dad into letting me date?

i think my daughter must have sent in this question! I can't tell you how to talk your dad into letting you date. That goes against "The Code of Fathers With Teenage Daughters." We dads have to stick together!

Seriously, if you promise not to tell my daughter, I'll tell you the best way to break down your dad to let you date (assuming you're old enough, which for me means you're 25, finished with grad school, etc. I'm *supposed* to say I'm only joking about that!). Here goes: The best way is by demonstrating that you are a responsible person.

You probably think your dad is overprotective, but he really doesn't want to micromanage every aspect of your life. That takes too much time and energy. And besides, what your dad really wants (other than for you to be saved in God's kingdom) is for you to be happy.

(I, by the way, am not overprotective—my wife is. She worries about wimpy stuff, like my children riding on roller coasters, and my taking them jet-skiing when I can't swim. I, on the other hand, reserve my worry for truly frightening stuff, like teenage boys.)

Your job is to make your dad feel comfortable with letting you out of *his* comfort zone. Think about it from his/our side for a moment. Dating *does* carry some risks. You are asking someone (your dad) to allow you to do something (dating) that carries the potential for harm, when his job until now has been to protect you *from* harm.

Dads aren't ready for a step like that unless you demonstrate that you are responsible. That means doing what you're supposed to when you're supposed to do it.

And it means not allowing your friends to influence you to do wrong.

Sooner or later your dad will let go of you; dads usually do (now, mothers are another story). You just have to help him get comfortable with the idea.

"HE'S FIVE YEARS OLDER THAN I AM"

Do you think it's OK for a 14-year-old girl to date a 19-year-old guy?

H'mm. Let me think about that one for a moment. OK, I've thought about it—*no!*

I'm wondering what I would do if someone five years older than my 16-year-old daughter tried dating her. Since I don't think the editors will let me say "He'd be a dead man," I'll start my answer from another angle.

During the teen years there is just too much difference in maturity between a 14-year-old (who is just entering her teens) and a 19-year-old (who is legally an adult).

Looking at it another way, someone who is 14 could still be a student in church school, while someone who is 19 could be starting their third year of college.

I am very uncomfortable with the idea of a 14-year-old involved with someone that far from their age. The opportunity for manipulation of the younger person is just too great. You'd be much better off dating someone your own age.

"I'M FOUR YEARS OLDER THAN HE IS"

I'm an 18-year-old girl. Do you think it's all right if I date a 14-year-old guy? I look young for my age, and people often think I'm in my midteens.

Recently I received a question from a 14-year-old girl who asked if I thought it was all right for her to date a 19-year-old guy. After my blood pressure came back down from imagining what *I'd* do if I discovered my daughter dating some guy five years older than she is, I answered the letter.

Basically, I told this young lady that the difference is just too great between the maturity levels of a 14-year-old (someone young enough to be in elementary school) and a 19-year-old (legally an adult). There's too much opportunity for manipulation of the younger person.

To answer *your* question, I still think the maturity gap between a 14-year-old and an 18-year-old is too big for a relationship to be a good idea. And because girls usually mature faster than guys, the maturity gap is even greater if the *guy* is four years younger than the *girl.*

There must be an attraction between you and Mr. 14-year-old, but I'm having a hard time understanding it. Let's get real—at 14, where can this guy go on a date? And even if his parents did let him date, he can't drive. So does this mean you come and pick him up?

And where does he get the money to fund dates (he probably doesn't have a job)? I would think this situation would put a lot of pressure on a 14-year-old guy.

I remember when I was in college and dated someone seven years older than I was (I was 20—she was 27). I never told my parents about it. (Though I'm sure my mom will read this book and find out now!)

Nothing bad happened, but I *always* felt awkward even to this day, and that was 1,000 years ago. I just don't think these kinds of relationships are a good idea.

"MY PARENTS WON'T LET ME HAVE A BOYFRIEND YET"

Why don't my parents want me to have a boyfriend? I'm 13.

My daughter is a few years older than you, but I don't want her to have a boyfriend either!

Now, when she's 25 and graduated from law school (she wants to be a lawyer), she can have all the Adventist boyfriends she wants! At that point I'll *want* her to have boyfriends, and if she doesn't have one, I'll find her one. She's not staying with me and spending all my money forever!

Seriously, there are a couple things you should remember that will help you get along with your parents.

First, in all likelihood your parents love you and want you to be happy. One thing that's helping me survive my daughter's teenage years is that she really believes I love her and want her to be happy.

That doesn't mean I don't get my share of "Daddy, that's not fair," "Daddy, you're being unreasonable," "Daddy, you don't understand," and "Daddy, you're being overprotective." (I don't know where she came up with that idea!)

But I'm very blessed by the fact that my daughter will probably think to herself, *Daddy's really going off the deep end on this one, but I know he loves me, and I know he wants me to be happy. I also know he's not going to change his mind, so maybe he's right after all.*

Now, that's a revolutionary idea to you teenagers—that your parents actually might be right about some things. But hello—your parents are older, more experienced, and, at this point, more educated than you are. You want your parents' trust, but right now you will have to trust your parents, which leads me to my next points.

I'll just be blunt. Too many of you equate having a boyfriend or girlfriend with kissing and all that. Now, I know that's not the only thing you think about when you think of boyfriends or girlfriends. But for many of you, that's part of it.

If I told you 15- and 16-year-olds that you could have a boyfriend or girlfriend but you couldn't touch him or her, you'd fall out laughing. Well, pick yourselves up off the floor. The earlier you start activities that are designed for sex, the harder it will be to avoid sex.

Let's be practical. Say you have a boyfriend at 13. What can you do together? You can't go on dates, because neither of you drive.

He can't drive over and see you, even if your parents would permit it. (If your dad is like me, your boyfriend isn't getting in the same area code as you at age 13!)

Would you really want his parents to drive him over to your house while your parents sit there with the two of you? You don't think they're going to leave you alone, do you?

Wait a little while longer.

"SHOULD I LEAVE MY BOYFRIEND FOR COLLEGE?"

I've just graduated from high school, and I have a chance to go to an Adventist college in another part of the country. The problem is that I don't want to leave my boyfriend. He says we can have a long-distance relationship. I love him, but I think that will be too hard. I mean, he's already not been completely faithful to me. Should I trust him and try to make it work?

I'm not going to tell you what you should do; I'm going to trust your judgment. But I'll tell you some of your options and some likely scenarios.

First, I'll admit that my blood pressure increased when you said, "I have a chance to go to an Adventist college . . . but I don't want to leave my boyfriend."

What I hope you meant was "I don't want to leave my boyfriend, but I am." A choice between a boyfriend and a Seventh-day Adventist college education is really no choice at all.

Besides, I would hope that if your boyfriend is also college age, he'll be going off to an Adventist college too. Not having some kind of post-high school degree nowadays is almost suicidal in terms of finding a good job.

And even if you do find a good job without a good education, you still don't have a whole lot of options. Suppose the job ends? Suppose you get a new boss whom you can't stand?

Make sure you have options, which a good education provides. I've seen people without a good education have good jobs and make good money, but when circumstances changed at their jobs, they were just out there with no options.

We're rapidly getting to the place where you really need a postgraduate degree. In many fields a college degree isn't even enough. So thinking about not going to college (and you probably weren't thinking of that) isn't a good thought at all.

Yes, you *can* go to college and have a long-distance relationship with your boyfriend. I've seen that kind of relationship work sometimes, but not very often.

I think that if you're going to go to an Adventist college, you should at least go there with your eyes open.

And quite honestly, keeping a long-distance relationship with Brother Boyfriend sounds kind of risky. You say that he already hasn't been completely faithful to you, and you were right there with him.

He's not likely to stay faithful to you hundreds of miles away. And unless you're willing to take a big risk with him, I'm not sure you have a lot of choices.

"WHEN SHOULD I GET MARRIED?"

After finishing college, should there be a period of time before I get married? Does it matter?

I got married four months after I graduated from Oakwood College. That was more than 20 years ago, and I'm still happily married. But even though it worked for us, I wouldn't recommend what we did.

My wife, Jill, had one quarter left of college when we got married. She finished, but it was a lot harder than we thought it would be, and it took much longer than we'd planned.

Jill moved from her parents' house into our house after the honeymoon. She never lived alone.

I didn't either. In those days the officials of the conference I worked for *strongly* "discouraged" young unmarried pastors from living alone. My conference president, a very nice man who has since retired, discouraged me by telling me I *couldn't* live alone.

So I lived with a family that consisted of the lady of the house and her three daughters, plus two unmarried ladies, both relatively close to my age. Now that I look back on it,

I'm not sure what would have been more prudent—living alone, or living with six females.

But the owner of the house treated me like a son, and I never thought about the fact that I probably wouldn't recommend this living arrangement to a young intern coming up.

Anyway, there's a certain independence that one gains from living on one's own. My secretary, a young lady just out of college, recently moved into her own apartment. She says she thinks it's important for a young woman to be out on her own for a while.

I think she's right. It would probably be good if a year elapsed between the time you moved out of your parents' house and the time you moved in with your spouse.

Who NOT to Bring Home to Mom

"MY GUY IS BAD NEWS"

Why is it that I like a guy who is not spiritual and doesn't like me, but I don't like the one who is spiritual but does like me? Help!

First of all, spirituality may not be *the* deciding factor in whether or not you like or don't like those young men. Even though a person is spiritual, that doesn't mean that's the person for you. You may be unattracted to that person for reasons other than the fact that they are spiritual.

For example, if something were to happen to my wife and I became single again and started going out with someone who wanted to have children, that would pretty much end it for me, even if she were the most spiritual being on earth. I am out of the having children business (technically, I guess I never was *in* the *having* children business!). I'm too old for diapers and 2:00 a.m. feedings.

I'm more concerned with you liking someone who is "not spiritual" than I am with you *not* liking someone who *is* spiritual. While spirituality is not the *only* thing, it is the *most important* thing.

In my opinion, few individuals will influence where you will spend eternity more than the person you pick as your life's companion. Since that person is almost certainly going to be a person who comes out of your dating life, you have to be careful about whom you let into your dating life. That person needs to be spiritual.

Don't let people *into* your life who are not helping you ultimately get out of *this* life.

"WHAT'S WRONG WITH DATING NON-CHRISTIANS?"

What's the problem with dating non-Christians?

The biggest problem for me is that the Bible says not to do it!

It's interesting that we place all kinds of requirements on the people we date—he's got to be older than I am, he's got to have a car. But God gives us only two requirements: the person cannot be married to anyone else, and the person's got to believe what we believe ("Do not be yoked together with unbelievers" [2 Corinthians 6:14]). That's all God requires, but many times we have a hard time with those few requirements.

Why did God say not to become unequally yoked? Well, first of all, we have to get to the place where we love and trust God enough so that even if we never understand *why* God says something, we do it *because* He says it. We will never understand why God says all He says; that's where faith and trust enter the picture.

But I think I understand *why* God says we should "not be yoked together with unbelievers." Because relationships are built on compromises. You get what you want

WHO NOT TO BRING HOME TO MOM

part of the time; I get what I want part of the time—give and take.

Believe it or not, there's even some give and take in your relationship with your parents. Do you really think your parents agree with everything you do, even if they let you do it? Of course not.

When my son, R.J., was 11, he decided to let his hair grow into an "Afro." As far as I was concerned, Afros went out 15 years ago. I couldn't stand his haircut, but I let him wear it, just as his friends did. (Here's a tip: never try persuading your parents to let you do something just because your friends are doing it—that's very bad reasoning. And don't try talking your parents into letting you wear an Afro. Of course, for many of you, that's not really a problem!)

Anyway, healthy relationships survive on compromise. But for a Christian, *whatever* God says cannot be compromised.

"Thus saith the Lord" is nonnegotiable; it controls every facet of a Christian's life. So inevitably there will come clashes between what the non-Christian feels should be compromised and what the Christian feels he or she *can't* compromise.

This puts Christians in a difficult position. Should they please someone they care about very much—even love— or should they please God?

Too many times people choose to please the other person at the expense of pleasing God.

Now, I know you young people are saying, "I would *never* allow myself to choose a boyfriend or girlfriend over God!"

But if obeying God is your priority, why are you dating a non-Christian in the *first* place? God plainly says in 2 Corinthians 6:14, "Do not be yoked together with unbelievers."

Every Christian who becomes romantically involved

with a non-Christian says they won't compromise their beliefs for the sake of maintaining a relationship. But the truth is, by dating a non-Christian you've *already* compromised your beliefs. Inevitably more compromise will follow.

A second key ingredient in making relationships work is a willingness on the part of both individuals to make the other person happy. I can't think of too many things I won't do in order to make my wife happy—even if those things make me *unhappy*.

For example, I hate shopping. But periodically I'll shop with my wife. Sometimes I'll even go on Sunday afternoons. That means I might miss my beloved football or basketball game on TV—to do something I hate for someone I love.

Now, if I'm willing to do that for my wife, you better believe Christians will do things in order to please non-Christians with whom they are involved. And when the other person isn't a Christian, inevitably some of the things that please him or her will displease God.

"WHAT ABOUT DATING CHRISTIANS OF ANOTHER FAITH?"

I really like someone who is a Christian but not an Adventist. Why shouldn't we date non-Adventist Christians?

We've said that Christians shouldn't date non-Christians, because the Bible clearly states: "Do not be yoked together with unbelievers" (2 Corinthians 6:14). Now we'll tackle the reason Seventh-day Adventists shouldn't date non-Adventist Christians.

I have young people tell me, "My boyfriend/girlfriend

is not a Seventh-day Adventist, but he/she is a Christian. So he's/she's not an 'unbeliever.'"

But I believe that a Seventh-day Adventist romantically involved with anyone who doesn't share their beliefs (an "unbeliever" in the seventh-day Sabbath and the health message and so on) is unequally yoked. In fact, I've found that the more the non-Adventist Christian is committed to his or her church, the more unequally yoked the non-Adventist and the Adventist tend to be!

That's because you have two people who profess commitment to belief systems that have some beliefs in common but have others actually opposed to each other. For example, you might believe something very strongly (keep the Sabbath day holy) that conflicts with something your dating partner believes equally as strongly (worship on the first day of the week). That's called unequally yoked.

Typically the Adventist expects the non-Adventist to yield his/her beliefs. The Adventist says, "I will *never* compromise!"

Maybe. But didn't the Adventist *already* compromise when he/she began a relationship with a person after the Lord warned, "Do not be yoked together with unbelievers"? The second compromise (and third, fourth, fifth . . .) is always easier.

"I HAVE A CRUSH ON MY TEACHER"

I have a crush on my math teacher. Do you think I have a chance?

Whether you have a chance or even *should* have a chance to begin a relationship with your teacher depends on whether these assumptions are true:

1. Your math teacher isn't married.

2. Your math teacher is reasonably close to your age.

3. Your math teacher is a Seventh-day Adventist.

4. Your math teacher is male and you are female, or vice versa.

Even if all these assumptions are correct, though, a teacher/student relationship is virtually impossible because everybody you know is going to oppose it. It will be even tougher yet if the teacher is female and you are male. I'm not saying that this kind of relationship is wrong; I'm just saying that it's unusual and more difficult for people to accept.

Back to the assumption list. If assumptions 1 through 4 are true, then my fifth assumption is that your dad is not like me. If one of my children's teachers tried dating them, I'd march into the education superintendent's office and ask if there were any openings for this teacher in another school (say in Outer Mongolia or Antarctica)!

Now that we've dealt with some assumptions, let's deal with some realities. First, if you have a crush on your teacher, you must ask yourself a somewhat painful question: What's the likelihood that my teacher will feel the same way toward me?

Let's get real. The likelihood isn't great, if for no other reason than that very few teachers can survive people knowing that they are dating a student, even if the situation takes place in a public school.

And if it happens in an Adventist academy, then *Hello?* The sound you just heard is your teacher's career blowing up and, as my conference president would say, "going down in flames!"

All right, I'm going to be blunt with you now. If you're attending an Adventist academy and your teacher dates you while you're still a student, he/she is *toast*! And yeah, not ordinary toast, but Texas toast, with Stripples on the side.

Unless you like rejection, it's going to be tough on you

to have feelings for someone who almost certainly can't respond. Even if they *do* respond, wouldn't you question a person's judgment who would torch their career for love? I know it sounds romantic, but it's crazy.

Or maybe, in order to have you *and* a career, you both decide to have a secret relationship, which is *really* bad news! A student involved in a secret relationship with a teacher is not a good idea at all.

The best thing you can do is ask the Lord to help you find someone with whom you can have a relationship that won't cause you (and them) all these problems.

"I'M IN LOVE WITH MY FOSTER BROTHER"

My adopted parents are also foster parents. They've recently taken in a 16-year-old guy. We've started going out. My mom doesn't know, because if she did, she'd kick both of us out.

I've prayed about this many times. I don't know how to show God to this guy. Even though he's a druggy, I still love him—his inner person. How can I lead him to God?

Should I let my parents know? Should I stop going out with him?

When I read your letter I said, "WHOA! This young woman raises all kinds of issues. A secret relationship . . . with a non-Adventist young man . . . who's into drugs . . . *who lives in her house!"*

As the father of a teenage daughter myself, the thought of that combination sent me into a cold sweat! That is not to say I don't sympathize with you. The human heart is a funny thing.

But here's a rule of thumb in relationships: If you can't tell your parents about it, it is almost certainly a bad idea. My daughter and I talk all the time. She tells me stuff even when she knows I'm going to say (usually loudly), "WHAT! You mean to tell me . . ." (These conversations are almost *always* about teenage boys.)

But still we can always talk. It's good for both of us. You need to talk to your parents. They need to understand what a difficult position you are in when they bring a teenage boy to live in their house.

Second (and last), you need to ask yourself if this relationship is making you a better person spiritually, emotionally, and mentally. That's what relationships are supposed to do—help make you a better person. Ask yourself honestly, "While I'm trying to 'lead him to God,' where is this guy leading me?"

"IS HOMOSEXUALITY WRONG?"

Is it wrong to practice homosexuality or bisexuality?

The Bible says it *is* (see Leviticus 20:13 and Romans 1:26, 27, to name just two references). No matter how much homosexuals try to rationalize it, practicing homosexuality is a sin.

But what we straight people have to realize is that *any* kind of sex outside of marriage is wrong (and I would include masturbation, another subject that pops up in my mail). Too many straight people seem to want to define homosexuality as the ultimate sin. They act as if there's a special place in hell reserved for homosexuals.

Yes, God says that homosexuality is an "abomination"—and it must be, because He says so. But He also says that "lying lips" are an abomination. That is *not* to equate homosexuality with lying, but to try to bring balance between the two extremes.

One extreme argues that practicing homosexuality isn't wrong. I heard a preacher say, "Homosexuality is a holy gift from a holy God." I don't think so. God approves of sex only between a man and a woman, and *only* if they're married to each other.

The other extreme says that practicing homosexuality is the ultimate sin and that AIDS is God's plague against homosexuals, His "terrible swift sword." One columnist wrote that homosexuals have "gone against nature," so AIDS is God's way of turning nature against them.

But AIDS can be contracted in ways that have *nothing* to do with sex. And while homosexual sex is the leading cause of AIDS in the United States, the leading cause in some other countries is *heterosexual* sex.

That's why telling anguished young people who think they may be homosexual that they're "cursed by God"— while not saying anything to the heterosexual with 20 partners—seems out of whack to me.

But what do you do if you find yourself attracted to someone of the same sex? There are no easy answers, but there *are* answers.

First, face the reality that if you're tempted to have sex with someone who is (a) not married to you, and (b) the same sex as you, it's wrong. Don't even try to rationalize it or romanticize it.

Maybe you feel you're "in love" (I'm not going to debate whether you really are or not, because that's beside the point). And you may feel that your thoughts and feelings are pure and natural.

But the Bible says in Romans 1:26, 27 that those feelings are *not* natural. That doesn't mean you should go around feeling subhuman because you have those feelings. No, they're *not* natural according to the Word of God, but I also think that God didn't naturally design heterosexuals to feel the things we do sometimes.

Those of you who find yourselves tempted toward same-sex relationships must come to grips with the fact that, biblically speaking, that's just not going to fly. If you're tempted to go in that direction, realize that you cannot. This realization is important, because Christ can't help us until we admit that we need something done.

Second, recognize that temptation is not sin—*sin* is sin. While being attracted to someone of the same sex is a problem, the attraction *itself* is not a sin. It's what you choose to do about it.

I suspect that the devil uses the guilt that comes with the *temptation* of homosexuality to stir up feelings such as *I'm a terrible person for even feeling like this. So because I'm such a terrible person and I'm going to be lost anyway, I might as well go ahead and act on it.*

Remember, just because the devil tempts you to sin doesn't mean that you *have* sinned. When the devil tempts you, you can get the help you need to overcome *any* temptation—including homosexuality and bisexuality. (If a person engages in sexual activity with *both* sexes, known as bisexuality, then he/she is engaging in same-sex activity *some* of the time. So he/she is practicing homosexuality at least part of the time.)

There are helpful resources available for homosexuals and also for their family members. Now, please do not misunderstand me—I'm not downgrading anyone because of their sexual orientation. I'm not saying homosexuals need help because *I* think they need it. I'm sharing this information because of the anguished letters I receive *asking* for help.

It's hard for me to read the letters I receive and not have some compassion for those struggling with homosexuality. They *know* that not many people (including their family members) are willing to accept a gay lifestyle.

So if they "come out of the closet" and are openly homosexual, that's not *really* socially acceptable. If they "stay in the closet," they have to live a lie. That sounds difficult to me. So at least some homosexuals need help coping with their situations.

My recommendation is to first seek the Lord and then seek the help of a competent professional Christian (preferably Adventist) counselor. Thanks to Elvina Wolcott of Adventist PlusLine (1-800-732-7587 or www.plusline.org), I've included a list of organizations designed to help people grappling with homosexuality.

While no group works for everyone and humans can't promise guarantees, I still want to provide this information. Remember, no one who has the faintest faith in the power of God is hopeless!

RESOURCES

Organization/Address	Comment
Someone to Talk to Newsletter P.O. Box 13354 Mill Creek, WA 98082-1354	Bimonthly publication. Help for parents of homosexuals.
Redeemed 3315 San Felipe Road, No. 134 San Jose, CA 95135	Support and confidentiality from Christians.
Exodus International P.O. Box 77652 Seattle, WA 98177-0652 Phone: 206-784-7799	Support for those overcoming homosexuality.

Organization/Address	Comment
Regeneration Books P.O. Box 9830 Baltimore, MD 21284-9830 Phone: 410-661-4337 Fax: 410-661-0284	Affiliated with Exodus. Provides books/ literature dealing with homosexual healing.
Homosexuals Anonymous Local chapters	A 12-step program.

Hot 'n' Heavy

"HOW FAR IS TOO FAR?"

How far physically can a girl go with a guy before going too far?

i suppose teen girls have asked this question (and caused their fathers' hearts to "fail them for fear") since Adam's day. What I understand your question to be is: How much kissing, touching, "petting," etc., can I do before it's considered wrong or dangerous?

I'm not going to tell you what's right and wrong with kissing and touching, etc., because the Holy Spirit is more qualified to deal with that than I am. But I will deal with the question How much can my boyfriend/girlfriend and I do before we run the risk of going too far?

My answer? Not much.

This whole discussion reminds me of the "Be responsible when you drink" theme the alcohol companies developed a few years ago. They promoted the idea "Know when to say when" (in other words, "Know when to say 'That's enough'").

"It's OK to drink," said the producers of those drinks,

Models: Not subjects of questions.

"as long as you drink *responsibly*." (And what else were they going to say—"Stop drinking, or the stuff we're selling you will *kill* you"?) How can you "drink responsibly," though, when alcohol affects the very part of you (your brain) that *tells* you when to quit?

Does everybody who drinks become an alcoholic? No. But no one becomes an alcoholic without taking that first drink. And no one becomes an alcoholic on purpose.

A large percentage of people who do drink get drunk, at least once. And too many drunk people climb into cars and kill themselves and/or other innocent people, making drunk driving crashes one of the leading causes of death. Sounds like a risky activity to me.

Just like drinking, kissing, touching, and petting are high-risk activities. People do these activities, in large part, because they feel good when they do them. Yet people tell themselves that they will voluntarily stop doing what feels good, while it *still* feels good, *just before* it gets them into trouble. Does that make sense to you? It doesn't to me.

Does all kissing, touching, petting, etc., lead to sexual intercourse? No. But kissing, touching, and petting are acts of foreplay that are designed to prepare the body for intercourse.

Consider the riskiness of assuming that you and your boyfriend or girlfriend are going to do things that feel good and prepare the body for sex, but you'll *always* stop *just before* having sex.

This kind of behavior sounds risky to me. You know, and I know, that there are a bunch of people who've gambled on the fact that they could "stop" kissing, touching, petting, etc., before having sex—and they lost.

"WHY IS SEX SO TEMPTING?"

Why is sex before marriage so tempting and so easy to do if it's wrong?

First let's establish one thing—sex before marriage *is* wrong because the Bible says it is. See 1 Thessalonians 4:3-7 for example, and remember that in the Bible "fornication" and "sexual immorality" usually mean premarital sex. I'm sure you believe that sex before marriage is wrong, but part of your question *did* say "*if* it's wrong." It *is*.

Now, *any* temptation is easy to give in to, at least to some degree. If there were no pleasure in sin, who would sin? Temptation, by definition, is a desire to do something that usually is wrong. If you don't want to do it, then it's not a temptation.

Sex is a particularly difficult temptation because it's pleasurable. I'm saying—as delicately as I can—that sex has a certain good feeling. Now, I know this is going to embarrass my daughter, who insists on thinking about her parents as nonsexual beings (as I'm sure many of you view *your* parents—that's how I viewed *mine*). But come on, if parents really were nonsexual, they wouldn't be parents, right?

There is a certain enjoyment in sex. And people don't easily stay away from what's enjoyable and pleasurable.

Teenagers think it's comical when I say, "It's a good idea for teenagers to avoid kissing." But if you kiss your boyfriend or girlfriend and it's good, why wouldn't you want another kiss? And another one? After a few of those knock-your-socks-off kisses, your body begins preparing itself for intercourse, because whether you want to admit it or not, kissing is part of foreplay. *Yes, it is.*

Now, foreplay may not be your intention, but your body doesn't know that—it's all revved up like a race car.

Then you tell yourself to stop.

Let me give you an example that will help you understand where I'm coming from. Let's say it's winter and you live up North. You're driving 80 miles an hour on an icy road, and a stop sign looms in front of you. You try slamming on your brakes.

You won't stop in time, will you? You should have started slowing down a long time before. Or better yet, you should have stayed at home.

Avoiding premarital sex is hard because too many people try to go too fast on a road that they *know* is slippery. Then they try slamming on their brakes at the last possible moment. Too many times young people (and older people) wind up crashing.

"HE WANTS TO MOVE FASTER"

My non-Adventist boyfriend and I have been going out for a year, but he thinks we should be "moving faster" than we are. I'm 14, and I'm feeling kind of embarrassed because everyone else my age is at the point where their parents let them go on dates to the movies and stuff.

But while my friends are at the movies, I have to go to church. I want to invite my boyfriend to my church's activities, but I don't know. What do I do?

You have more than one problem!

First, even though I know everyone's tired of hearing me say this, I have to say it again: you're "unequally yoked." And that's a big problem!

You and your boyfriend believe different things, have different interests, and so on. That's evidenced by the fact that you've been going together for a year, and you still don't feel comfortable asking him to your church.

Think about this for a second: you don't seem to have a problem going with him to the mall, or wherever you can go out with someone when you're 14. Your boyfriend asks you to go to secular events with him, so why can't you ask him to go to church with you?

By now I'd think he'd know how important your God and your church are to you. If he knows they're important to you and still isn't interested in them, doesn't that say something about him? And if he doesn't know how important your God and church are to you, *why* doesn't he?

Relationships are to a large extent about sharing your life, goals, and interests with someone. If you can't do that, you'd better take a serious look at this relationship. The problems you're encountering, though, are too typical of being "unequally yoked."

Now, I'm also concerned that you're a 14-year-old young lady with a boyfriend saying that your relationship should be "moving faster." First, I'm not comfortable with you going out at 14, at least not without a group and lots of chaperons!

But what exactly does he mean by "moving faster"? I've heard this line before, and too many times it's another way of saying "I think we ought to be moving toward having sex."

If that's what Brother Boyfriend means, then you *really* have a problem. (Though not as big a problem as Brother Boyfriend would have if you were *my* daughter!)

I certainly think you need to be "moving faster"—"moving faster" toward the door!

"WHAT'S WRONG WITH PREMARITAL SEX?"

What's wrong with having sex before marriage, as long as you're only sexually involved with one person?

The first reason sex before marriage is wrong is that God says it is. That reason alone is enough for me.

But let me give you *another* reason sex before marriage isn't a good idea.

STDs. You can contract all kinds of sexually transmitted diseases, including the AIDS virus.

As a pastor I've watched members of my church die of AIDS on two occasions. And it wasn't a pretty sight.

As I visited my AIDS-stricken members during their illness, I saw the disease completely overtake their bodies. I watched one member cough such violent, wracking coughs that it seemed as though he were about to cough up his *insides*. Later, this individual coughed up blood—projectile blood, shooting out of his lungs and mouth as if coming from an out-of-control water fountain. Shortly afterward, he died.

No sexual experience is worth going through *that*. Having sex isn't worth losing your life, especially losing your life to a disease that's so terrible that dying may seem better than living.

And don't tell me, "I'm not going to get AIDS, because I'll 'protect' myself."

Hel-lo? "Protection" isn't even guaranteed to keep people from getting *pregnant,* let alone from getting AIDS. Do you *really* want to bet your life on your "protection"? Please.

Besides, do you *really* think you'll *always* use "protection"? Most "protection" requires that you stop right in the middle of some passionate activity, think about what you're doing (if you were *really* thinking, you wouldn't be engaging in premarital sex), and then put on "protection."

Now, are you *really* prepared to bet your life and your future on the chance that you'll *always* stop and "protect" yourself *every* time? That's a *serious* gamble.

Years ago (even before *my* time) a TV show aired called *You Bet Your Life*. That's exactly what you're doing when you have unprotected premarital sex (and once you start having premarital sex, the odds are good that you *will* have unprotected sex—at least once).

Now, the way you've worded your question makes it sound as if premarital sex might be OK if you're involved with *only* one person. But that assumption presupposes that the *other* person has been involved with only you. Good luck finding *that* out!

Besides, as I've said, if you're engaged in premarital sex, you're likely to have unprotected sex sooner or later. In that case you'd be sexually involved with not only every person your partner has ever been involved with but with all of *their* partners as well. So if just *one* person in that equation has a sexually transmitted disease, you're at risk.

So just to have sex, you bet your life. Doesn't sound really smart to me.

Another reason you shouldn't have premarital sex is because of the risk of pregnancy. You absolutely *do not, do not* want to have children before you're ready.

Having children even when you're happily married is frightening. And having children when you're not married is positively scary!

Now, make no mistake about it, I *love* my two children. And losing them would be the single most horrible thing that could happen to me—next to losing my soul.

But the *next* most horrible thing that could happen to me would be for me (well, not *me*, but Mrs. Edmond) to have *another* child now—especially a little girl! I mean, by the time that little girl became a teenager (if the Lord hadn't come yet), I'd be too old to chase the teenage guys away. I guess I'd have to get some kind of souped-up wheelchair to help me do the job—and I would!

Anyway, children—at least *my* children—give more than they take, but they *do* take. In general, children take your time, your energy, and *especially* your money!

Children, even good ones like mine, basically operate on the premise that parents exist for the sole purpose of giving them whatever they want as soon as they want it. OK, I'm exaggerating a *little,* but not much.

Sadly, the majority of people involved in premarital sex don't think they'll get pregnant, get anyone else pregnant, or get AIDS. But I must say to all of you who argue "It can't happen to me"—"Oh, yes, it *can* happen to you!"

This country is full of people dealing with unplanned pregnancies and sexually transmitted diseases—people who "didn't think it could happen to them."

Most people tend to think that bad things happen only to other people. But the reality is that in a sinful world, bad things happen to even *innocent* people and *even more so* to people who engage in risky behavior.

But even if you don't get pregnant, get anyone else pregnant, or contract a disease, you *still* pay a high price for having premarital sex.

From talking to young people who've become involved in premarital sex, I've learned that one of the high prices is guilt. You feel bad about what you've done, especially at first.

And—I've heard this more than once—it's much harder to resist sexual temptation once you've started having sex. This is the case not only for you but for your partner.

For example, once you've had sex with someone, it's much harder for him or her to believe you if you start saying "No." Can you *really* mean you don't want to have sex *ever* again until you're married—after you've already had it?

So, besides all the other consequences, premarital sex changes your relationship and the way you look at your partner forever.

It's just not worth it. God knows that, and that's why He doesn't want us to do it.

"IS MASTURBATION OK?"

Is masturbation OK? Doctors say it's harmful, Ellen White says it's harmful and sinful, but the Bible doesn't really say.

When I started writing an advice column for *Insight* several years ago, I anticipated having to answer questions about controversial subjects such as interracial relationships, homosexuality, and masturbation.

Sure enough—the questions came. We did a three-part column on interracial relationships and another three-week column on homosexuality. And now for that other topic I knew would show up in my mail eventually (and it did)—masturbation. Is it wrong?

Well, let's look at the facts. Ellen White is pretty unfavorable toward what she describes as "self-abuse." In essence, masturbation is a form of sex—with one's self. "Self-sex," if you will.

In masturbation there is sexual stimulation, gratification, and at the end, climax. As far as I'm concerned, that's sex. And biblically speaking, sex with *anyone* other than one's own spouse is wrong.

Now, I realize that not everyone is going to agree with that definition. Just as not everyone is going to like me dealing with this subject at all. Believe me, I'd rather not deal with it either. But it's out there. You and I know that.

And our job is to deal with it from a Christian perspective.

So here are a couple points to keep in mind regarding this subject:

1. If masturbation is a sex act committed with one's self (and I think it is), then it's wrong.

2. Sex is an act of giving to one's spouse. Masturbation is not about giving at all—it's about gratifying one's own sexual desire. It has nothing to do with anybody but the person involved in the act.

A person (even a married person) who approaches sex as nothing more than an act to gratify his or her own desires is a dangerous partner. Is anyone attracted to people who think sex is only about what *they* want, what *they* need, or what feels good to *them?*

That is not the kind of person you want to *be* or *be with.*

"I'M ATTRACTED TO EVERY GIRL WHO WALKS BY"

I'm a teenage guy, and I'm trying to be a Christian. Yet I find myself feeling attracted to every young woman who walks by. Sometimes I feel like I want to have sex. I don't want to feel this way—what should I do?

Well, you're probably a lot more normal than you think you are. Sometime during a guy's pre- or early teenage years an increased sexual awareness and sexual drive kicks in. That's just the way things are. (And that's why fathers of teenage girls are the way *they* are.)

As I've said before, it's not a sin to be *tempted.* Temptation isn't sin; *sin* is sin. It's what you do about the temptation that counts.

So what can you do about feeling sexually attracted to

every woman who walks by? Most important, don't dwell on those sexual thoughts. As soon as the devil puts them into your head, pray, asking God to take them out of your head.

If you dwell on the temptation, you'll start fantasizing about it. Then it'll start to look good to you—temptation *always* looks good. But it never looks as good *after* you've sinned as it looked *before* you sinned.

So don't dwell on the temptation or fantasize about it. As I said, it'll look good to you, and then you'll start to think of reasons you should give in to it. The human mind that's not surrendered to God can *always,* absolutely always, think of good reasons to sin.

I heard Elder C. D. Brooks say in one of his sermons, "When you decide to follow your desires, you can talk yourself out of the church and into hell, and it will make sense to you all along the way. You can be lost, and think you're right."

He's correct. So the best way to deal with temptation is through prayer, and then by removing the temptation or moving away from it.

Also, there are great benefits to staying busy, especially doing things for others. If you don't have much to do, the devil will find *something* for you to do. Minds that aren't active are places upon which he can plant *his* thoughts, *his* ideas, and *his* agendas.

The next time the devil tempts you with thoughts about sexual impurity, remember this: nothing that comes from the devil is free. If you follow his suggestion, he might give you a reward that will last a few minutes. But after the reward *always* comes the regret.

"WHY DO GUYS WANT SEX?"

Why do guys always want to have sex before marriage?

Well, I'm not sure I completely agree with the premise of this question. If I really thought all guys wanted to have sex before marriage, I'd lock my teenage daughter up!

Also, this question implies that premarital sex is always the guy's idea—that he seduces the girl, and she never seduces him. I don't believe that.

Having made these points, let me tell you some of the basic differences between men and women (even though some of my feminist friends might disagree). If you don't understand these differences, you can get into trouble, whether you're a guy or a girl.

Generally, men (particularly young men) are more quickly aroused sexually than women. Men are also more "sight-stimulated"—more easily aroused by what they see.

Every time I say this, some woman replies, "That's old-fashioned. When we see a good-looking man with his shirt off, we become aroused too."

That might be true. I'm not a woman, so who am I to argue?

I certainly recommend that if you're a woman and a man tells you something about men—listen! If you have an older brother and he tells you that your skirt is too short, listen! (And if your father tells you, *really* listen!) This also works the other way. Fellows, listen to your sisters and mothers. They can often see things about girls you can't.

So I won't argue with women who say they're aroused by a good-looking man with his shirt off. I will say that a woman who goes around topless doesn't even *have* to be good looking to cause sexual arousal. Usually males tend to get aroused by exposure to a lot of female flesh, and it often doesn't matter who the female is.

This may be hard for women to understand, but generally it's easier for a man to separate sex from love. While both sexes have sexual desires, a girl's desire is likely to be more limited toward her boyfriend, while guys are more likely to want to have sex with a girlfriend *and* other females. Guys can become sexually involved with someone for whom they have no other feelings.

Sex seems to be more of an emotional experience for women—a giving experience. It's not safe, ladies, to give yourself to a man except in marriage. One reason is that you'll have a very hard time knowing whether the man is with you to satisfy his sexual desire (which he can satisfy with virtually any other woman), or because he loves you.

So, ladies, if a guy wants to become sexually involved before marriage, tell him, "Before we say 'I do' in a marriage ceremony, we don't."

"MY GIRLFRIEND WANTS SEX"

What if my girlfriend wants sex, but I don't? What do I do?

Run! While men are allegedly the stronger sex, I don't believe that's true when it comes to sex. I believe there are very few men who are able to resist a woman determined to have sex with them if that woman is around them for an extended period of time.

Now, that's no excuse for you fellows to "fall" the next time some woman throws herself at you. And just because a woman throws herself at you doesn't mean you have to "catch" her! But it does mean you're going to have to, as one of my friends says, "get out of the dodge."

There are a couple ways you can deal with temptation. You can stand there and try to fight it off, or you can get away from it. Personally I favor the get-away-from-it-as-though-your-clothes-were-on-fire approach, *especially* when it comes to sexual temptation. There are a whole heap of folks out there who thought they could handle sexual temptation, but wound up "biting the dust."

Don't misunderstand me. There is *no* temptation that cannot be overcome, because the Lord promised that He will not let us be tempted beyond what we can bear (1 Corinthians 10:13). There's always a way out, but when it comes to sex, let's face it—most unconverted people don't *want* a way out.

So why put yourself through all that, my brother? Find someone who doesn't want to have sex before marriage, or find a young lady whose father will do bodily harm to her and you if you don't control yourselves!

I hear there are still a few fathers like that around.

"HOW CAN WE CONTROL OURSELVES?"

How can we control our bodies so that we are not tempted to have sex?

What you need to control more than your body is your *mind.* That's because I believe sexual temptation begins in the mind. If the Holy Spirit rules your mind, then your mind will rule your body.

The converted mind controls the eyes, for example. So avoiding sexual temptation means that you cannot look at everything and everyone. This is particularly important for young fellows, because men tend to be considerably more "sight-stimulated" than women.

Another key to handling sexual temptation is to recognize how difficult it is *to* handle. The best way to handle sexual temptation is to avoid it as much as possible. Too many people try to see how close they can come to having sex without actually having sex. Relatively few young people want to acknowledge that the activities in which they like to engage—kissing, touching, caressing, etc.—are in reality acts of foreplay designed to prepare the body for sexual intercourse.

Now I realize that sexual intercourse is not what many of you intend to happen when you kiss someone or touch them. But those activities *are* foreplay, and foreplay, generally speaking, is designed to lead to intercourse.

Then add to that the tendency of some young people to follow the latest style in dress (which for young ladies means having outfits barely less revealing than some lingerie).

Now you have a situation: two people . . . alone . . . with a strong physical attraction . . . They are engaged in activities designed to prepare the body *for* sex, and then they *wonder* why they are having a hard time not *having* sex.

The final contribution to sexual dynamite comes with the tendency of too many young people (and older people) not to take God seriously when He says "Be not unequally yoked." Think about it, young people. How many non-Christian young people do you know who are *really* committed not to having sex under *any* circumstances before marriage? Not many; some, but not many.

If you are dating someone who does not believe sincerely that premarital sex is wrong, how are you going to resist sexual temptation? If only one of you *wants* to say no, that sharply reduces the odds of no actually being said.

The bottom line is that if you continue walking a sexual tightrope, you will fall sooner or later.

"WHY CAN'T I FIND A NICE GUY?"

I can't seem to have a long-term relationship with a guy without him wanting to have sex. Why can't I find the right guy who doesn't want that?

Again I find myself in the position of defending teenage guys—a strange position for the father of a teenage daughter! But even *I* don't believe there aren't *some* nice guys out there who don't want to have sex before marriage.

If you keep running up against the *other* kind of guys, maybe you ought to do a little self-examination. Not that I believe that every time some hot-blooded, hormone-filled guy hits on a girl it's the girl's fault. I *don't* believe that at all.

But the only person you can ever *make* change is yourself. So it's always good to look at *yourself* after someone makes an improper advance toward you. (It's also good to tell your father about the guy. Then, after you tell your *father,* tell the *guy* to start running!)

Be honest, and ask yourself a few questions:

1. Should I have been with this guy in the first place? Sometimes you have advance warning about what a guy wants. I've had ladies tell me that guys asked them to have sex. The ladies said no, yet they stayed with the guy *anyway!* Do you think that just because you said no (but stayed with him), he's not going to ask again? Please.

Oh, he might *tell* you that he understands and respects your beliefs. (If he *really* respected your beliefs, why did he ask in the *first* place?) But what do you expect him to say? Do you *expect* him to tell you, "I hear you *saying* no; but I'm going to wear you down"? If he's asking, that tells you where his *mind* is—his *body* is soon to follow.

2. Was I appropriately dressed? You can certainly get

hit on when you're wearing a dress—as my secretary puts it—"down to your ankles and up to your neck." Modesty doesn't guarantee that a guy will act properly.

But ladies, *stop* telling yourselves that how you dress makes no difference, that it's no one's business but yours. That's *complete* nonsense.

Sometimes what I see young ladies wear shouldn't be called a "dress"—it should be called "undress." It looks like some of my wife's nightgowns!

And let me be diplomatic but honest. As a married man, I *know* what I was thinking when I bought my wife's nightgowns. What I want to know is: What were *you* thinking (and I *really* want to know what your *parents* were thinking) when you bought that dress that looks like lingerie?

If you dress provocatively and someone does indeed become "provoked," if you dress for sex and someone then *asks* you for sex, well, that's partially on you *as well as* on him. Wake up, ladies.

"WHY DO PEOPLE ACT PROUD OF LOSING THEIR VIRGINITY?"

Why do people give away their virginity and act as if they're proud of it?

I'm not sure that everyone who gives away their virginity is proud of it, though I'm sure some are. The ones who tend to be proud of it, more often than not, are males.

Ladies, I hope it hasn't escaped your attention that there's a definite double standard when it comes to sex. If you're a male who has a lot of sexual partners, that's *supposedly* a good thing. To the world you're considered "virile, manly, a stud." But not so for females.

Years ago I read a book written by a man who was at that time a very famous basketball player. (Though if I mentioned his name, only about half of you would be anything more than vaguely aware of who he was. Famous today, forgotten tomorrow—there's a spiritual lesson in that.) Anyway, this man claimed to have had sex with 20,000 different women.

Now, forget for a moment how unlikely that is. First of all, who knows that many women? And second, was he keeping some kind of tally sheet somewhere?

I know I said to forget it, but I can't. If this guy *really* had sexual relations with 20,000 different women, that would mean that in 30 years of adult life he would have had to sleep with 666 new women every year. That breaks down to more than 10 different women a week, and almost two different women every day. Not likely!

When people heard Brother Famous Basketball Player's claim, they thought that either (1) he was lying, or (2) he was a major stud.

I guarantee you that any woman who claimed to have had 20,000 different sexual partners wouldn't have been called a stud. More likely people would have called her a name that started with the same letter! That's a double standard, ladies, and it does exist. Remember that.

So, yeah, some people do give away their virginity and then brag about it. But not everybody does.

What do you expect people who've thrown away their virginity to say—if they decide to say anything at all? "I lost my virginity, and I'm ashamed"?

If you're ashamed of something, you don't want to say anything about it. So people who brag about promiscuity either *have* no shame, or they're compensating for their shame by *pretending* to have no shame.

I'll say again what I've said before: no matter how good the devil makes temptation look, he never tempts you with any reward that doesn't later offer regret. The short-term pleasure you might get from following the devil's way is never worth the eventual and inevitable pain.

"WE'VE MESSED UP—NOW WHAT?"

My girlfriend and I messed up. We went too far and ended up having sex. We feel really guilty about it, but it's hard to resist. We're not virgins anymore now, though, so what does it matter?

The first part of my response deals more with the people who are where you once were—virgins, but not sure they want to stay that way. If that fits you, please know that there are more people who engage in premarital sex and regret it than you would imagine. Too many people think that virginity is nothing special—until they don't have it anymore.

So if you're out there trying to decide whether or not to stay a virgin, please remember this: If you give up your virginity before marriage, you will very likely regret it, even if you *never* get pregnant, cause a pregnancy, or get a sexually transmitted disease.

If premarital sex was such a great idea, a loving God would not have said (and said very emphatically and repeatedly), "Don't go there. In fact, please don't even *think* of going there."

But suppose you've already "been there." Suppose being a virgin is no longer an option for you.

I believe in the power of God to restore and re-create. No, He can't give you your virginity back, but He can give you a relationship with Jesus, which is even more important than having your virginity. Moreover, He can give you the power not to fall into that sin again, and that's important.

My experience in dealing with young people has shown me that a very big problem with premarital sex is that once you yield to it the first time, you're much weaker in that area thereafter. In other words, a bigger problem than losing your virginity the first time is the ease with which you acquire a taste for premarital sex. Once the barrier to premarital sex is broken down, it seems to be a hard barrier to put back up.

But the Lord can help you to do just that. He's done it for many people, and He can do it for you. You just have to ask Him and then, like Jacob, hold on to God until you get the victory.

And you will get the victory. You probably won't gain victory easily, but you will gain it.

If you ask God to come in and take over, He'll fix it so that not only will you *not* be having premarital sex—you won't even *want* to have it anymore.

That's the power of the God we serve.

When It's All Over

"HOW DO YOU HANDLE AN EX?"

How do you handle an ex-boyfriend or ex-girlfriend?

Well, most people use one of three basic approaches. The first is the vengeful, vindictive, treat-your-ex-like-a-dog approach. (Although I wonder where the expression "Treat someone like a dog" comes from. My wife loves her dog, and she used to buy her dog presents at Christmastime. That kind of treatment doesn't sound so bad, does it?)

I'm ashamed to tell you that I used this vengeful, vindictive approach during my teenage years. You didn't want *me* for an ex-boyfriend. Being vindictive made me *feel* good, but now I realize that it made me *look* bad, particularly if I wanted to get back with my ex-girlfriend.

During academy I was on the drama team. The small team consisted mainly of my girlfriend, me, and another couple. When *both* couples broke up at the same time and all of us had similar ideas about our exes, you can imagine what a fun group *we* were!

Aside from the fact that a vindictive, vengeful approach

isn't Christlike, it's not very smart, either. All you're really doing is confirming in your boyfriend or girlfriend's mind that it was a good idea to break up with you in the first place.

Approach number two is just a variation of the first—ignoring your ex. I tried this approach too. Believe me, it's just as bad an idea as the first approach for the same reasons.

Approach number three works best. Be polite and friendly, but back away so you can get on with your life (which you have to do anyway). Move on, but be nice about it.

"WE'VE BROKEN UP TWICE"

I have a boyfriend; we've been together for five months. I've already broken up with him twice, and we're back together. I want to break up with him again, but I don't know how to do it.

Let me see if I have this straight: you've broken up with the same guy twice. You don't want to be with him anymore, but five months later you're still with him. If you aren't careful, while you're trying to figure out how to break up with him (again), you'll wind up marrying him!

I can't read your mind, but it sounds to me as if you can't decide what you like the least—being *with* your boyfriend or being alone. I'm guessing you like being alone the least.

But if that's true, is that really fair to your boyfriend? Would you want to be with someone who said, "I don't really *want* to be with you anymore, but being with you is better than being alone. I'll hang with you until something better comes along"?

I don't think you'd want anyone doing that to you. So don't do it to anyone else.

Probably the only way you two are going to get away from each other is to make a "clean" break. No more phone calls, no more dates, no more anything. You can be polite, but that's about it. Any prolonged exposure, and you'll end up together again.

"HOW DO YOU STOP LIKING SOMEONE?"

How do you stop liking someone you've had a massive crush on but still like them as a friend?

First, you need to be honest with yourself. There are different feelings a person has for their friends, and different feelings a person has for their boyfriend or girlfriend. Do you know which you feel for this person?

I always operated on the premise that it's very hard to continue hanging around an old girlfriend when the relationship is over. If I wanted to get over how I felt about that girl, I had to move on. I couldn't spend time talking with her on the phone or going places with her. I had to pretty much quit "cold turkey."

Of course, you have to be polite and friendly. I must confess I didn't always do that, but acting ugly isn't going to bring them back. Trust me; I know. Besides, you only make yourself look bad.

Be nice to the person you're trying to get over, but move on. Time heals all wounds; you *will* get over that person. Then it will be easier to be friends.

"MY EX WON'T LEAVE ME ALONE"

What do I do when an ex-boyfriend won't leave me alone? I have no feelings for him anymore.

Let's be realistic: all boyfriend/girlfriend relationships end sooner or later. They end at the altar, where boyfriend and girlfriend become husband and wife; or they end because one or both parties involved decide it's time for the relationship to end. The second way is how most relationships end.

I'm not sure that most of you reading this *should* be involved in a relationship, but if you are, be realistic. In all likelihood, you're going to break up fairly soon. Consider this your wake-up call; you and your boyfriend/girlfriend will almost certainly break up, and it almost certainly will hurt one or both of you.

Now, since you're probably going to break up, it would be nice if you both stopped having feelings for each other *at the same time*. But that's not likely to happen.

What usually happens is that *one* person decides that the relationship is over, and the other person wants to keep it going (even if he/she doesn't admit it). The adjustment is most difficult for the person who is sort of "left behind." He/she wants to hold on to something that no longer exists.

Now that you understand why your ex-boyfriend is acting the way he is, remember this: be kind and honest—one day you'll probably be on the receiving end of this situation.

Kindly but firmly let your ex know that it's not possible to continue the relationship. Tell him that your feelings are no longer the same. And if your feelings have changed because there's someone else, you probably need to say that, too.

Don't give your ex the old I-need-to-spend-more-time-with-my-schoolwork speech, then hang around someone else the next day. Being lied to makes the person hurt worse.

After your talk, cut off the constant contact. Some people like the company of their ex—they just don't want the commitment. But that makes it harder for the ex. It often gives him/her false hope when he/she really needs to move on with life. Be polite, but be gone.

If the unwanted attention persists, then you need to think about getting some adult help.

"MY SUMMER ROMANCE ENDED"

I met a guy at camp last summer and fell in love with him at first sight. We became good friends right away, and it got to the point where we held hands and he kissed me on the cheek. I didn't want the week to end, but it did. I gave him my phone number and e-mail address, but he still hasn't contacted me. I keep hoping he'll call. Now I feel like our time together was a waste. I love him, but I don't know if he feels the same way. What should I do?

Virtually everyone's familiar with camp (or camp meeting) romances. There are always people who come to these events with the goal of having a relationship with someone while there. And sometimes they have no intention of the relationship surviving beyond the week.

Other people simply get all caught up in the thrill of finding someone to share those special times with. And that's not all bad.

I remember my camp meeting romance. I was about 14 or 15, and her name was Yvonne. We met on Thursday and went to the bonfire that night. I spent the next two days of camp meeting looking for her, but I never found her.

Eleven years later in Michigan I ran into someone who looked familiar. We started talking, and she told me where she lived and about her family. Suddenly it hit me—this was Yvonne!

I said, "You don't remember me, but I'm Dana Edmond. We met at camp meeting in 19—." (I don't dare give you the year!)

Then she recognized me and said, "I never forgot you."

I hadn't forgotten her either. Now, if we were in Hollywood, we would have gotten back together. A lost love found, an old summer flame rekindled!

But we weren't in Hollywood, and by this time I was happily married. Yvonne got married later, and the last I heard, she had about 9 million children.

That's how our relationship ended. And what's wrong with that? We didn't do anything wrong. At the time both of us thought it would develop into something more. But it didn't.

The only thing that came of that evening was good memories. And life is made up of good memories, at least in part.

No, he didn't call you, and it doesn't seem as though he will. But that doesn't take away from the nice time you had (though as a father, I'm not crazy about the hand holding and cheek kissing!).

It wasn't a waste. It was like most relationships you'll have as a teenager—a learning experience and a stepping-stone.

Maybe *your* story will have a Hollywood ending. Imagine being separated for 11 years. Then you two meet by chance in Michigan, start talking, and discover that he *lost* your phone number and e-mail address (it happens!). But he never forgot you. Neither of you are married, and *you* can get married and have 9 million children (if the Lord doesn't come first).

"DISTANCE CAME BETWEEN US"

I dated a guy long-distance for almost a year. We got to see each other once a month, and we always had a great time. He was my best friend, and we really loved each other. But then he broke up with me without explaining why.

After that we tried being "just best friends" for a while. But we got into an argument one day, and then he refused to be anything to me anymore. I kept calling him, but he wouldn't talk to me. Finally I gave up.

That was two months ago. Last week I found out through a mutual friend that he still likes me and still talks about me. I'm confused because he hurt me a lot, but I still love him. What should I do?

This is a tough question in some ways, because it's obvious that you're hurting. It's clear to me what you have to do, though. (That's only because I'm not the one who's hurting. You are, and I'm sorry.)

To answer, let's look at some basic facts.

Fact 1: No matter how wonderful teenage relationships are, most of them end sooner or later. And because one person isn't usually ready for the relationship to end, *somebody* usually gets hurt.

Now, people can try to *pretend* that they aren't hurt when someone breaks up with them (guys tend to do this more than girls). But having someone break up with you usually hurts. Why wouldn't it? If you didn't care about the person you were with, why were you with them in the first place?

So breaking up is (a) pretty inevitable, and (b) pretty painful.

Fact 2: You were even more vulnerable to a painful breakup because yours was a long-distance relationship. I'm not saying you shouldn't ever have one; I'm just saying that you need to be realistic about the fact that long-distance relationships usually don't work out.

I don't like saying what I'm about to say, because I feel like some sort of "relationship scrooge," but here goes. I know that all of you young lovers out there think it's going to last forever and you'll never get hurt. But it's probably not going to last, and eventually you (or your boyfriend or girlfriend) *will* get hurt.

Hurt is the toll that almost everyone pays on the "relationship highway." The only sure way not to pay this price is not to get on the highway.

But thankfully, time heals wounds. And during this healing process you'll learn things about yourself that you wouldn't have learned otherwise.

After the hurt is gone, you'll still have the good memories. I had some pretty spectacular breakups in my younger days, but what do I remember now? Mostly the good times.

Experiencing hurt makes you more sensitive to someone else's pain. That's a big part of why Jesus, the Son of God, became the Son of man. Having lived on earth, He understands our pain.

Now, what do *I* think you should do? Consider these facts:

Fact 1: If you were to get back together with this guy, it would still be a long-distance relationship. And it would still carry the same "crash" risk.

Fact 2: This guy still hasn't told you why he broke up with you in the first place. Is there someone else? Can he just not handle a long-distance relationship? If I were you, before I thought about getting back together with this guy, I'd like to know why he broke up with me in the first place.

Fact 3: While there are two sides to every story, Brother Ex-boyfriend doesn't sound like he treated you very well after your "argument." He didn't return your calls, and just sort of "dissed" you.

Suppose you get back together and have another argument? Or suppose you get back together and he decides to break up *again,* without giving you a reason *again?* Are you ready to go through what you've already gone through *again?*

Fact 4: He hasn't told you that he still likes you—your mutual friend said that. Suppose your mutual friend is wrong?

If your ex-boyfriend does still like you, he needs to say that to you. In fact, he needs to say a lot of things to you. And until he does, it's over.

"I DIDN'T TELL HIM TILL IT WAS TOO LATE"

I met a guy last year who came to my school as a foreign exchange student for one year. We became friends, and I really liked him. But I didn't tell him about my feelings because I didn't want to hurt our friendship. Now he's returned to his country, and I've written him three letters, but he's written back only once. It hurts, and I just can't seem to get over him. How do I get over him?

If I had an easy answer to that question—"How do you get over your feelings for someone when the relationship is over?"—I'd be rich!

But your question raises a couple issues I'd like to

address. First, you say you didn't want to let this guy know how you felt about him while he attended your school. Even when you knew he was leaving soon, you still played the guess-how-I-feel-about-you game.

Now, this may come as a shock to those of you who read my column in *Insight* regularly and know that I'm hopelessly old-fashioned about a lot of things. But ladies, I think it's OK to let a guy know that you like him.

You don't have to chase him or throw yourself at him, but what's wrong with letting him know that you like him? If you *do* like him but succeed in making him think that you *don't* like him, what do you expect him to do? Pursue you *anyway,* even after you've acted as if you have no feelings for him? That doesn't make sense.

Would *you* pursue a guy who tried to get you to think he didn't like you? Of course not.

Just so you know, I gave this same advice to my daughter just before she started dating her boyfriend. I told her, "Don't play games. Don't make him unsure of how you feel about him."

And she listened. (I *also* told her not to say this to him until she was 25 and out of law school. But she *didn't* listen to that part.)

Now, let's talk about how you can "get over" this guy. It's true that time eventually heals pretty much everything. But I also think that you should ask the Lord to heal your hurting heart. He will.

Also, ask Him to help you learn from this experience, because you'll probably go through something similar again. It's part of growing up.

In the meantime, don't beat yourself up because this guy isn't sending you letters—many people are terrible about writing letters, even when they care about the people sending them letters.

And even if this guy were writing back to you, the best

relationship you two could have would be a long-distance one—a *really* long-distance one. And those usually don't work anyway.

"I CAN'T LET GO"

I'm 17, and two years ago, when I was 15, I started going with a guy who was 25. But now he hasn't contacted me in two months, and I think it has to do with the last time I saw him.

I went over to his house, and one thing led to another. We didn't go all the way, because I'm not ready to have sex, but I think he was upset.

I know I have no business messing around with him, but I believe I've fallen in love with him, and I can't let go. And now I'm afraid that my parents might find out, because he's not a Seventh-day Adventist, and they're *very* strict. What should I do?

Start running away yesterday! Do you have a few hours to hear all the dangerous things about your relationship? All right, here are the big ones:

1. The age difference. If I were 25, a non-Adventist, and had a girlfriend, I'd expect to have sex with her sooner or later. No, not *all* non-Adventist guys expect sex. But studies show that the average young man loses his virginity around age 17.

I think your boyfriend is mad because he expected you to have sex with him, and you stopped before you did. (Thank God!) But if you keep putting yourself in situations like that one, you're *toast.*

2. He's not an Adventist. You have different value systems. For example, you think premarital sex is wrong, and he doesn't. It's hard *enough* to do right when both of you are Seventh-day Adventist Christians.

Do you *really* think you can stay with this guy *and* stay pure? I don't want to hurt your feelings, but you can stay a virgin *or* you can stay with this guy. *You can't do both.*

3. Your parents don't know. If you have to sneak behind your parents' back to do something, that "something" is almost always the *wrong* thing. If you keep seeing this guy secretly, you're going to either get pregnant or get caught.

Are you *sure* you want this relationship? You have to sneak around, you turn him down for sex, and he doesn't call you for *months*. I know you think that other people are keeping you apart, but if this guy wanted to see you, he'd find a way.

Get him out of your life. Anyone who hasn't contacted you for two months is *already* out of your life. But if you should see him, adopt the "nothing but polite conversation" rule.

Put this guy in your past, or he'll destroy your future.

Tough Stuff

"I LIKE MY FRIEND'S GIRLFRIEND"

What should you do if you like your best friend's girlfriend?

There are several things you can do. And you've already done the first two things I'd suggest: first, admit that you like your best friend's girlfriend, and second, realize this isn't a very good idea.

The mistake many people make in this kind of situation is that they don't admit—even to themselves—that liking their best friend's girlfriend is a *problem*. Some guys go into denial, telling themselves, *I don't like her*. Yeah, right.

When you like someone, often other people can sense it. There's just some kind of chemistry between two people when at least one of the parties is attracted to the other. Usually *other* people can sense that chemistry too. You can't tell me you don't know when one of your friends likes someone.

For the past few years now, I've been listening to my daughter describe her relationship with various fellows like this: "We're just friends" or "He's my buddy" or (the least believable line of all) "We're like sister and brother."

I've heard her say that about people I *knew* she was attracted to or I *knew* were attracted to her. While she was busy denying the attraction (and while I was busy hoping there *was* no attraction), I could almost always tell when an attraction existed one way or the other.

The point is, if there's an attraction, admit it—at least to yourself, though probably *not* to your best friend, and *certainly not* to his girlfriend.

Second (you've heard me say this before), in relationships treat other people the way *you* want to be treated. This rule applies not only to girlfriends but to best friends, too. Would you want your best friend to move in on *your* girlfriend?

Stay away from situations that could get you into trouble and betray a friend's trust. Respect your best friend's relationship the way you would want him to respect the relationship if it were yours.

If you *don't* respect the relationship, it's a no-win situation for you. Because if you go after your best friend's girlfriend and "miss," chances are she's going to tell your best friend, who will then become your *ex*-best friend. And if you *do* get your best friend's girlfriend, you *still* lose your best friend (only to gain a girl who's proved she can't be trusted).

Remember, girlfriends (and boyfriends) come and go. But best friends can stay friends forever.

"HOW DO I CHOOSE BETWEEN TWO GUYS?"

How do I choose between my boyfriend and my best guy friend? I love them both.

've talked to young people in rap sessions, in question-and-answer periods, and in one-on-one counseling sessions. But I haven't heard this question many times.

You need to ask yourself some hard, honest questions. You have a boyfriend and a best guy friend, and you love them *both* the *same* way?

Feelings a person has for their boyfriend/girlfriend and their other friends aren't the same. You might be friends with someone, and then have a boyfriend/girlfriend relationship develop *out of* that friendship. Or you might consider your boyfriend/girlfriend your best friend.

But romantic feelings and platonic feelings are different. And whenever the two types of feelings get mixed up (whenever you tell yourself that what you're feeling is platonic when it really is romantic), you have a potential problem.

What it *sounds* like is that your feelings for your best guy friend may be deeper than you thought or are willing to admit. If you can't choose between your boyfriend and your friend (assuming that your boyfriend is not being unreasonably possessive and jealous), the problem may be that your feelings for your best guy friend run a little deeper than friendship.

A good rule to follow is to treat other people the way you wish to be treated. If the situation were reversed, wouldn't you want there to be at least *some* difference in the way your boyfriend treated you and felt about you—and the way he treated and felt about his best girl friend? Would you be comfortable if your boyfriend was as close to another girl as you are to your best guy friend?

You ought to be able to have other friends as well as your boyfriend, but if there's no difference between your feelings for your boyfriend and your best guy friend, you might end up losing both of them.

"BOTH BROTHERS LIKE ME"

What should I do if a guy my age likes me, and so does his older brother? I've told the older brother that I don't like him, and I've asked him to leave me alone. But how can I get him to really leave me alone without being rude to him?

Well, you left some things unsaid, which makes answering your question a little hard. You said that you've asked the older brother to leave you alone, but apparently you didn't ask the younger brother to do that. Is that because you like the younger brother?

If you *do* like the younger brother and he likes you— and if his older brother *knows* this, but still wants to get involved with you *anyway*—that says a lot about Brother Older Brother. And most of what it says isn't good.

I talked to some young ladies once about what they called "The Code." They explained that "The Code" is basically this: If a girl likes a guy, then all her girlfriends can't show any interest in him at all.

They can't be interested in him while he and their friend are *deciding* whether or not they're going to go together, *while* they're going together, *and* for a suitable length of time after they've *stopped* going together—as long as six months to a year!

I told these young ladies with "The Code" that they were "The Crazed"! They couldn't tell their friends to stay away from their boyfriend when he was *no longer* their boyfriend!

But then again, brothers and sisters ought to have a code or something that keeps them from risking a long-term relationship—a family relationship—for a short-term romantic one.

When you get to be as old as I am, you're going to have a hard time remembering even the *names* of some of your old flames. So how in the world could you risk a family relationship for a romantic one that will almost certainly be over in a matter of months?

The fact that Brother Older Brother would risk throwing away his relationship with his brother for you is flattering, but it's also frightening. It says something about his values and his sense of loyalty—that he doesn't have any.

You were right not to get involved with him. And if he won't take "No" for an answer, ask an adult to help you get your message across to him.

But I think you need to think hard about getting involved with Brother Younger Brother, too. Family opposition is a problem in any relationship. You have to decide whether or not this relationship is worth the risk.

"MY DATE'S FAMILY DOESN'T LIKE ME"

What if your boyfriend or girlfriend's family doesn't like you?

I remember when my brother and younger sister told my girlfriend, Jill (now my wife), that they liked my old girlfriend better. As the young people at my daughter's school would say: "The tactlessness!"

My brother and sister didn't mean any harm, but recently I got a letter from a girl telling how her boyfriend's sister turned ugly toward her. The sister called her all kinds of names, etc. If you're in the same kind of situation, here's what you should do.

Think about why your boyfriend or girlfriend's family might not like you. Is it just them? Or is it you? If your boyfriend/girlfriend has become less responsible, less spiritual, and less careful of grades since you started dating, maybe that's why they don't like you.

But maybe it's not you. Maybe your boyfriend's/girlfriend's family is wacky, and that's tough, because you can't change them. In that case your boyfriend/girlfriend should step in and defend you.

Boyfriends/girlfriends don't have to disown their family for your sake, but they shouldn't sit back while their family attacks you like hungry sharks. If they allow their sisters and brothers to talk about you, well, that says something about this person you're dating, doesn't it?

It's up to the people dating to "sell" their boyfriend or girlfriend to their families and serve as liaisons between them.

The first time my daughter's boyfriend came to our house, she gave me instructions. "Daddy," she said, "he's going to be nervous, and I want you to make him comfortable."

(Between you and me, I *wanted* Brother Boyfriend to be uncomfortable. I *wanted* him to think, *If I breathe wrong on Courtney tonight, I'm a dead man.*)

On the other hand, I knew my daughter was working on Brother Boyfriend. I imagined that she told him, "I know you've heard my dad say from the pulpit that he's building a trapdoor over a bottomless pit outside our front door. And I know he's said it's for the first boy who comes to see me before I'm 25, but he doesn't mean it."

It's easier to deal with your boyfriend's or girlfriend's family if your beloved sticks up for you. If your boyfriend/girlfriend can't or won't do that, before long your relationship will quite likely end up as *toast*.

"DO LONG-DISTANCE RELATIONSHIPS WORK?"

Do long-distance relationships usually last?

Some long-distance relationships last, but most don't. It depends on the circumstances.

Some time ago I visited a place where it's not uncommon for one spouse to live in one country while the other spouse lives in another. Of course, these out-of-the-country relationships tended to be limited to older (as in much older than me!) couples.

On the other hand, if you go to an academy or college and your boyfriend/girlfriend stays home or attends another academy or college, the odds are that your relationship is going to—as we say—"bite the dust."

No matter what you tell each other as you're saying goodbye, promising "I'll be faithful" and all, this is not likely unless one of you is attending an all-girl or all-boy school.

(By the way, if you're a girl attending an Adventist all-girl school, please let me know! My daughter will be enrolling there immediately!)

"ARE INTERRACIAL RELATIONSHIPS WRONG?"

Some people classify those involved in interracial relationships as "unequally yoked." Yet 2 Corinthians 6:14 talks about being "yoked together with unbelievers." This text seems to deal more with what a person believes (or doesn't believe) than their color.

However, there might be a broader meaning to

2 Corinthians 6:14 that covers other major differences between people (significant age differences, economic differences, educational differences, etc.). It's a good idea to avoid relationships in which there are significant differences, because relationships tend to thrive between people who have a lot in common.

Still, there's a difference between saying the relationship isn't a good *idea* and saying it's *wrong*.

It's tough to make the case that interracial relationships are wrong. Moses married a dark-skinned woman of another nation, and some of his family did not approve (see *Patriarchs and Prophets,* chapter 33). And when Moses' family gave him a hard time about it, God was not pleased and even struck Moses' sister with leprosy.

Yet if you date or marry (and presumably you *would* date someone before you married them) someone who isn't in your racial category, *somebody* you know and are close to will almost certainly disapprove. Even if your *parents* don't disapprove (and quite often they will), then someone else will disapprove, as my daughter would say, "for no good reason."

When I attended academy, 90 percent of the students there were White. I went from an all-Black environment to an almost all-White school in a White Conference in an all-White town.

One of my Black friends started dating a beautiful Hispanic girl. All the Black girls at the academy had paid this guy *zero* attention before. But as soon as he started dating this Hispanic girl, those girls slammed him big-time. *They* weren't interested in dating him, but they didn't want the *Hispanic* girl to date him either.

I believe that some (but not *all*) opposition to interracial relationships has *something* to do with bigotry. Bigotry isn't logical. It's based on fear and ignorance.

Often there's very little real contact between the races

in the Adventist Church. Yeah, I know you go to *school* together, but when was the last time you visited a church made up of people of another race when it wasn't a school-related function? Or when was the last time you invited someone of a different race over to your house for dinner? I thought so.

People tend to fear the unknown. And we have all these stereotypes of each other inside our heads. We live in a society that, though it has come a long way, still has a race problem. That's the world in which we live—a world in which some people are more concerned about whether your boyfriend or girlfriend *looks* like you than how they *treat* you. You need to be aware of this before you start an interracial relationship.

For some people, including some of your friends and family, it doesn't matter how educated, spiritual, refined, cool, nice, or *whatever* your boyfriend or girlfriend is. To these people *what* he or she is isn't nearly as important as what *color* he or she is.

Your parents know this. So even if *they're* not bigoted, their natural inclination is to try to protect you from people who are. Parents usually go for the safest choice, and interracial relationships aren't a "safe" choice. Your parents might oppose interracial relationships because they know the grief other people will likely cause you. You can't blame them for that.

So what do you do if your family opposes your boyfriend or girlfriend because of race? Try these ideas:

1. Be respectful. Even if you think your parents are bigots, respect their feelings. You want them to respect yours. Besides, being disrespectful of them won't change their minds.

2. Be understanding. In order to change people, you have to understand them—look at things from their point of view. You don't have to *agree* with them, but to come to a "meeting of the minds," you have to *understand* their point of view.

As you try to understand your parents, realize that *your* experience with people of different races may not be your parents' experience. Your parents may not have had *any* experience with other racial groups. If so, they might be relying on stereotypes. Or their experiences might not have been positive.

3. Be honest. Do you really like your Black, White, Hispanic, etc., boyfriend/girlfriend, *or* do you like the fact that it sends your parents into cardiac arrest? Rebellion isn't a good reason to start a romance.

4. Be smart. If you yell and scream at your parents over an interracial relationship and then sneak around behind their backs, you take the focus off their intolerant behavior and put it on your bad behavior.

5. Be patient and prayerful. If the Lord wants you two together, He'll work it out. If the Lord doesn't want you together, you don't need to be on the same *continent,* much less in the same relationship.

"HE WANTS ME TO JOIN HIS CHURCH"

I'm dating a guy who isn't a Seventh-day Adventist, and he wants me to join his church. Should I?

I don't want to be insensitive, but there's not a whole lot to discuss here. You can't join your boyfriend's church—not today, not ever.

Either the Seventh-day Adventist Church is the remnant church of the Bible prophecy, or it is not. If it's *not,* then we should all leave it today!

But I absolutely believe that it *is.* So even to ask "What should I do?" and suggest leaving your church tells me how harmful your relationship with this guy is.

I've said this on a number of occasions, but I'm going to say it again (even though I know that some of you like what I have to say *less* each time I say it!). Those of you involved with non-Seventh-day Adventists need to know that you're unequally yoked. That means that your relationship is *wrong* according to God's Word, and you need to get out of it—now.

I know that's strong medicine, and while I hope it didn't hurt anyone's feelings, I feel it needs to be said. No matter how much we try to rationalize such a relationship, God says *don't* do it (see 2 Corinthians 6:14; Amos 3:3; Deuteronomy 7:2-4, etc.). And when we *do* what God says *don't* do, it's *wrong.*

If you think what I just said was harsh, read Nehemiah 13:23-27, *especially* verse 25. You'll see that what I said was mild compared to what Nehemiah said and *did* about these kinds of relationships.

I know that some of you will try to argue your way out by saying that those Bible texts apply to marriage. I'm sorry, but I don't buy that. I know way too many young adults who are *marrying* outside the church who *wouldn't* be if they hadn't *dated* outside the church.

What all you we'll-date-'em-but-we-won't-mate-'em people are proposing is equivalent to my leaving Nashville, Tennessee, and going north on I-65 to go to Oakwood College in Alabama. I *should* have gotten on I-65 going south, but I tell myself, *I know I'm going in the wrong direction, but I'll turn around before it's too late.*

If you *know* you're going in the wrong direction and you're not "planning" to continue, *why are you going that way in the first place?*

Now, let's not go down the my-mother-dated-my-father-before-he-became-an-Adventist-and-she-won-him-to-the-church road, either. Something *good* coming out of something *wrong* doesn't make the wrong right.

I bet that if I had all of you in a room and said, "Everybody here who's ever had a relationship with a non-Adventist, would you please stand?" I suspect a bunch of you would stand.

Then if I said, "How many of you during that relationship *never* compromised your principles and beliefs—would you remain standing?" I suspect there would be a lot *fewer* people standing.

Yes, I know some of you are thinking, *You can compromise your principles when dating Adventists, too.* That's sad but true. It's also beside the point.

If you're compromising your beliefs while dating *Adventists*, the solution isn't to start dating *non-Adventists*. The solution is to *stop* dating until you can date *and* be true to your principles and to God.

While you're thinking I'm hopelessly old-fashioned and out of touch, I'm going to dig myself in a little deeper and say that I hold parents responsible for some of this "problem."

Now I'm really in trouble. While I surely don't wish to hold up myself as some model parent, I've told my daughter (and I'm about to tell my son, who is now a teenager) that under *no* circumstances will I allow her to date a non-Adventist. Nor will I *automatically* allow her to date someone just because he's an Adventist.

I realize that sounds bigoted and narrow-minded to some of you. But I want my children to be saved—that's my *number one* agenda item. And I know that one major factor that impacts my children's salvation is the people they have relationships with up to and including marriage.

So anyone—Adventist or not—who doesn't have an eternally positive impact on my children will face big-time opposition from me. That's my role as a parent.

"I'M IN A VERY SMALL TOWN"

I'm a high school student, and I go to a small church in a small town. There aren't a lot of young ladies in my church to date. What do I do? The Bible says we aren't supposed to be unequally yoked, but being located in a small town cuts down on my choices a whole lot. And what about those people who've dated outside the church and converted their boyfriend/girlfriend?

Occasionally I get a question I haven't heard very often, and this is one of them. Actually, I've heard this question, but usually from ladies who say there aren't enough men in the church. Since you're a young fellow, that makes the perspective different.

But I really think you're saying there aren't a whole lot of people of *any* gender in your small church. So what should you do?

Certainly a lot of people reading this can identify with your situation: a small church with few young people. But do you remember who first recognized the fact that it's no fun being alone?

He's the one who, after creating Adam, declared, "It is not good for the man to be alone. I will make a helper suitable for him" (Genesis 2:18).

God created a desire for companionship in us, and even His Son felt the need for human companionship when He lived on earth. Though He had the company of God the Father and the angels, Jesus said to His disciples in the Garden of Gethsemane, "Stay here and keep watch with me" (Matthew 26:38).

I believe God understands your desire for companionship, and He's definitely not against it. But He is against your filling that need in the wrong way.

111

That's where we come to your second question: "What about those people who dated outside the church and won over their boyfriend/girlfriend?"

Yes, it's sticky to make a case for not dating boyfriends/girlfriends who don't believe as you do, because there are situations in which someone dated and/or married outside the church and converted their non-Adventist spouse into the remnant church.

Do *I* know of situations in which an Adventist has dated outside of the church and won their boyfriend/girlfriend or husband/wife to Christ? Yep, sure do.

Do I know about *many more* cases in which the non-Adventist never came to Christ, or worse yet, "won" the Adventist *out* of the church? Yep. And you probably do too.

This situation is a lot like gambling. Sometimes you hit the jackpot, but most of the time the jackpot hits your wallet.

Does the fact that some people "convert" their companions make it OK to date/marry outside the church?

Some would say yes, but it sounds like "the end justifies the means" argument to me. Do we *really* believe that as long as things turn out OK in the end, we can do whatever we want?

I actually heard about a drug dealer who used to pay tithe on his drug profits. Later the drug dealer got converted, stopped selling drugs, and no longer had much money to donate to the church's treasury. Does that mean it's OK to sell drugs as long as you give some money to the church? No.

First and foremost, God wants us to love and trust Him enough to obey Him no matter what. When you think about it, every time someone converts his/her girlfriend/boyfriend or wife/husband, it emboldens others to become unequally yoked.

And the sad part is that most people don't convert their dating companion or spouse. In fact, many people are led *out* of the church by their non-Adventist date or spouse.

Let's be honest—dating and/or marrying outside the church is a big gamble on your relationship with the Lord.

Is your relationship with the Lord strong enough that a non-Adventist won't pull you out of the church, but you'll pull him/her in? Do you really want to bet your soul on that?

God said, "Do not be yoked together with unbelievers" (2 Corinthians 6:14). It *doesn't* say: "Do not be yoked together with unbelievers—except for you guys in small churches in small towns. *You* guys are off the hook."

So what can you do? First, remember that your loneliness, though troubling, is probably only temporary. You said that you're in high school. College awaits you, and at the average Adventist college there are numerous single Adventist young women.

In the meantime, the Adventist Church provides many opportunities to get together with Adventist young people from other churches. In my conference we have camp meeting, youth congress, youth federations, senior youth retreats, camporees, etc.

If you attend such functions (and too many young people in your situation—small church, small town—*don't* go), you'll increase your circle of friends (even if you don't find "Ms. Right"). Besides, if you did find "Ms. Right" at age 16, what would you *really* do about it anyway?

In the meantime, concentrate on *being* like Jesus, so that when He does help you find someone, you'll be a blessing to them. And remember, as hard as it may seem to be by yourself, it's better to be with *no one* than to be with the wrong *someone*.

"PEOPLE DON'T TRUST US"

Why can't certain people trust me around my girlfriend? They seem to think I'm doing something wrong.

One thing I constantly tell my son, R.J. (who's now a teenager!), is that you always have to conduct yourself in such a way that people will give you the benefit of the doubt.

I've been around a number of teenagers who've basically taken the position that they can do whatever they want, and if someone gets the wrong idea about them, well, that's the other person's problem. I've heard teenagers brag, "I don't care what other people think of me."

Well, that's not true. Few care *more* about what other people think of them than teenagers do. That's what peer pressure is all about.

So let's face it, what other people think of you *matters*. Now, what *they* think of you doesn't matter as much as what *God* thinks of you or even what you think of yourself, but it does matter.

Do you think that when you're looking for a job, it doesn't matter what the person interviewing you thinks of you? Of course it does.

Now, first of all, you must accept at least some responsibility for the fact that some people get suspicious of you when you're around your girlfriend. That doesn't necessarily mean it's your *fault* they're suspicious. Some people are just overly suspicious.

But it *is* your responsibility to conduct yourself in such a way that will give reasonable people no reason to be suspicious of you. And you should try to live so that even if people happened to run into you in a situation that might look questionable, they'd still give you the benefit of the doubt.

Let me give you an example. When I was a young pastor, I baptized a young lady who then backslid and started working as a waitress in a bar.

She hadn't belonged to our church for very long, so I didn't know where she lived. But I did know where the bar was. (Hey, it was a small town, with like one bar in the whole town.)

So since I had no other way to reach her, I went to the bar to talk to her. I parked *way* down the street (so no one would pass by and see the preacher's car in front of the bar!). Then, after looking over my shoulder about 100 times, I entered the bar to talk to my church member about coming back to the Lord.

Now, if one of the saints had seen their pastor coming out of Joe's Bar (or whatever its name was), I would have had some explaining to do! But I hoped that if someone did see me coming out of the bar, they'd consider how I lived my life and at least give me the benefit of the doubt. (Of course, they wouldn't *keep* doing that if I kept going to the bar!)

So here's my point: try to live in such a way that reasonable people (a) won't be suspicious of you, and (b) will be willing to give you the benefit of the doubt.

Now, what should you do if certain people just have negative impressions of you? First accept the fact that, at least to some degree, you're responsible for the impressions people have of you. And if those impressions are negative (even if it's not your fault), you need to try to correct them.

If certain people are suspicious of you when you're around your girlfriend, ask yourself: *Why? Is there anything I'm doing that may look or sound suspicious?*

Sometimes young people spend a lot of time complaining about how unfair it is that people are suspicious of them. And sometimes the suspicion *is* unfair.

But then I have to ask: "What are you going to do about the unfair suspicion besides complain about it? Is there any behavior that *you* need to change? Remember, you can change only your own behavior."

I'd suggest that you answer those questions too. And here are some more to ask yourself: "How do my girlfriend and I act around each other? Are we always all over each other? Can we sit together without touching each other all the time?"

If you and your girlfriend are always involved in "PDA" (when I was in academy, that's what the faculty called "public display of affection"—I think they *still* use that term!), then at least *some* of the time *some* people will wonder, *If they act that way in public, how do they act in private?*

There are enough suspicious people in the world, so don't bring suspicion upon yourself.

Here's another thing to keep in mind. People are less likely to be suspicious of you and your girlfriend if you demonstrate that you've found a healthy balance between an understandable desire for young couples to spend time together and a life that includes other people too. If you two spend every waking moment either with each other or talking to each other on the phone, or if everyone else is playing basketball inside but you and your girlfriend are alone outside in some dark corner, then, yes, people will get suspicious.

As I said before, there are some negative impressions that people get about us that we can't do anything about. But you ought to take responsibility for the ones you *can* change, and then change them.

"CAN I LEAD MY GIRLFRIEND TO CHRIST?"

How can I win over my non-Adventist girlfriend? She's in the tenth grade and is so sweet and loving. But she's from another Protestant denomination.

When she noticed that I would never accompany her to her Friday night parties, she asked why. I told her that, first, I don't drink, and second, it's the Sabbath. She was surprised but receptive.

So how can I lead her to Christ? If she accepts the Lord and His remnant church, we won't be unequally yoked.

Is it a good idea for Christians to be involved with someone they have to "lead to Christ"?

I have no doubt that your girlfriend is sweet and loving, but she parties every Friday night with people who drink (even though she's under age and her friends probably are too).

I'm not sure that Christians can do *right* linking themselves with people who are doing *wrong*.

Yes, young people (and older people) argue that they're attempting to "win their girlfriend/boyfriend" to Christ and His truth. But I have several problems with that argument:

1. It's not really honest. Was the thing that attracted you to your girlfriend *really* the desire to win her to Christ? When you first saw her, was your first thought about saving her soul? I didn't think so.

What usually happens is people use the excuse of winning souls as justification for a relationship they want. But it's difficult to win people to Christ and "the truth" if we're disobeying the part of truth that says, "Do not be yoked together with unbelievers" (2 Corinthians 6:14).

117

2. Suppose she does join the church. Can you really be sure she's joining the Adventist Church because she loves God, or because she loves *you*?

3. Suppose she doesn't join the church. Do you really want to fall in love with someone and then have to break up because she isn't a Seventh-day Adventist (which you knew when you started the relationship)?

That's really tough to do, which is why many people don't do it. It's much easier to tell yourself that the person will someday join the church than to face hard reality: in relationships like yours, the odds are greater that the non-Adventist will pull the Adventist *out* of the church than that the Adventist will pull the non-Adventist *in*.

A fellow by the name of King Solomon tried to convert his girlfriend. He was the wisest man who ever lived. He probably had an IQ of 500 and got perfect scores on his SAT and ACT.

But early in Solomon's reign as king he married Pharaoh's daughter, an unbeliever (1 Kings 3:1). The story appears to have a happy ending, though—Solomon's unbelieving wife "joined the church" (*Prophets and Kings,* p. 53). So Solomon's "small sin" of marrying an unbeliever didn't matter, right?

Wrong. The problem with small sins is that they don't stay small. Because Solomon successfully converted his wife, he apparently thought he could do it again. And again. And again.

Solomon's harem ultimately grew to 1,000 women—many of them unbelievers. Solomon might have told himself he was no bigamist. He was an *evangelist,* bringing beautiful women to Christ (and coincidentally, to his bedroom).

First Kings 11:4-6 relates the sad story that happened at the end of Solomon's life: "For it came to pass, when Solomon was old, that his wives turned away his heart after other gods: . . . for Solomon went after Ashtoreth the goddess of the Zidonians, and after Milcom the abomination of the Ammonites. And Solomon did evil in the sight of the Lord" (KJV).

One of the devil's best tools is to make wrong seem right. Yes, Solomon *did* convert his wife (the Lord in His mercy sometimes overrules and allows good things to happen when we make bad choices). But all too often we take the good things that happen when we make bad choices as God's *approval* of those bad choices.

Then we wind up making those same bad choices again. Or worse yet, *other* people see the good things the Lord sometimes allows to happen, and they feel emboldened to make those same bad choices.

As wise as he was, Solomon didn't realize that it's a lot easier for someone else to pull you down than for you to pull somebody else up. As wise as he was, Solomon couldn't handle being unequally yoked. I suspect that most of you can't handle it either.

Some of you think I'm wrong about that—maybe I am. But if I'm *wrong* and you listen to me, the most you'll lose is a boyfriend or girlfriend. If I'm right (I am, because I'm just telling you what God says) and you don't listen, you could lose your soul.

"WHY DOES LOVE HURT?"

Why do we continually get hurt by those we love?

My theory is that we can be hurt *only* by those we love. We get hurt, to a large degree, because we've given a part of ourselves to someone. We've made an "emotional investment."

That reminds me of my son's school basketball team. Last year they were competing in a tournament for small private schools across a part of Tennessee. Well, R.J.'s team made it all the way to the championship game, but lost just as the buzzer went off.

After the game I felt deflated, even though I was very proud of how my son and his friends had played.

But here's my point: while I was watching that game, to me it wasn't just a well-played game between two teams, as it may have been for some people watching. *My* son, in whom I've made an emotional investment, was out there playing!

If I hadn't had an emotional investment in one of the players and hadn't cared who won, I could have walked away and said, "What a great game!" But I agonized over that point scored at the last second by the other team—for my son's sake.

Now, he got over it (probably faster than I did!). And I think he learned from that experience—that life doesn't always go the way you'd like it to go, that you should show some dignity even when you lose, and that you should try again.

But the point is, when you invest yourself emotionally in someone or something—whether it's a girl or a guy or a basketball game—and you lose that someone or something, it hurts. It hurts because you gave of yourself.

And you gave of yourself because you cared about that thing. If you didn't really care, you wouldn't have invested in it, and losing it wouldn't matter. You can be hurt only by something or someone you care about.

Yet the good news about getting hurt is that you can almost always learn from it. For example, people may have tried to tell you that this guy or girl wasn't good for you, but you were so in love with being in love that you didn't hear their advice until that person hurt you.

Now, I don't want to sound all poetic about pain, like it's so wonderful—it's not. But pain can be a good thing.

My mother had a heart attack a few months ago. It so happened that Lori Peckham, the editor of *Insight,* was attending our camp meeting in Huntsville (where my mother lives) when it took place. Lori was good enough to go visit my mother, which I'll always remember.

But it was my mother's chest pains that told her she needed to go to the hospital. She did, got everything fixed, and is on her way to being as good as new.

If it weren't for the pain, she wouldn't have been aware of the problem. It was her pain that led her to the hospital to get the problem fixed.

Pain alerts us to the fact that there's a problem. And many times the pain in our lives leads us to Dr. Jesus, which is a good thing.

"DID JESUS EVER FALL IN LOVE?"

I know that the Bible says Jesus was tempted with everything we're tempted with. So did Jesus ever fall in love? Did He ever find a woman He wanted to marry? And if He didn't, wouldn't that mean that He really wasn't tempted the way we are?

No one's ever asked me those questions before! Let me deal with your last questions first, because they *may* be the easiest ones to answer.

The Bible says in Hebrews 4:15 that Jesus was tempted in all points as we are, yet He didn't sin. So I believe that since the Bible *says* that Jesus was tempted the way we are, then He really *was* tempted by the things that tempt us.

I'm old-fashioned like that: if the Bible says something, then I believe that it's true, even if I don't understand it.

For example, who can explain Jesus' virgin birth? Definitely back then a woman couldn't have a baby without having sexual intercourse, which automatically made her a nonvirgin.

But the Bible says, "Behold, a virgin shall conceive, and bear a son" (Isaiah 7:14, KJV). Now, I can't *explain* how that happened, but I *believe* it happened.

So when the Bible says that Jesus was tempted like we are, I believe it means that He was tempted with every *kind* of temptation that we're tempted with—not that He was tempted with exactly the same temptations.

Some of the temptations that we face weren't even around then. I mean, Jesus wasn't tempted to spend too much time playing video games. But I believe that He faced an equivalent temptation—whatever that may have been.

Now, the Bible doesn't say whether or not a female ever presented a problem for Jesus. It's quite possible that one did, though. Jesus was probably rather muscular from all His carpentry work, and we know He was a gentle and kind person. So it's very possible that someone found those qualities attractive.

But the Bible doesn't say anything about Jesus' love life. And therefore, I don't feel comfortable saying anything about it either. I just don't know.

I do know that the devil threw everything he had in his awful arsenal at Jesus. And ironically, I believe that Jesus faced some things that we'll never have to.

For example, it's about 9:00 p.m. on a weeknight, and as I'm writing this I'm a little hungry. But while I'm sure there are stones outside my office building, I'm not tempted to turn them into bread—I can't.

Another temptation Christ undoubtedly faced was whether or not to come down off the cross on Calvary. I know that if I'd been the one hanging there, I wouldn't have been tempted to come down—I wouldn't have had the power to.

But while Jesus had the power to come down off that

cross, He overcame the temptation in order to save us.

Now back in heaven, He wants to help us overcome temptation and to "save them to the uttermost that come unto God by Him" (Hebrews 7:25, KJV).

Parents

"THEY DON'T TRUST ME"

How do you let your parents know that you're trust-worthy?

I may be oversimplifying this, but the best way to let your parents know that you're trustworthy is to *be* trustworthy. You can't get your parents to believe that you're something you're *not*—at least not for very long.

Being trustworthy means that you have to do several things:

1. Be obedient. If your parents tell you that you can't do something—go out with a certain guy or girl, for example—then *don't* sneak behind their backs and do it anyway. When you sneak around you almost certainly will get caught sooner or later (usually sooner!).

And when you do get caught, two things happen (at least in my house). First, you end up in big trouble. Second (and even more important), you lose your parents' trust. Once trust is lost, it's very hard to regain.

I know that some of you think it's OK to sneak around if, in your opinion, your parents are wrong. But it's not OK.

Sneaking around is deceptive and dishonest. So even if your parents are wrong (and they're not wrong nearly as often as you think), deceiving them makes *you* wrong too. And two wrongs have never made one right—they just make two wrongs.

2. Be responsible. That means doing what you're supposed to do when you're supposed to do it, and especially being *where* you're supposed to be *when* you're supposed to be there. If your curfew is at midnight (or whenever), be home at midnight. In fact, be there a little *before* midnight. Don't try to see how close you can come to curfew. That's not responsible. And being responsible builds trust.

3. Be honest. Tell your parents the truth *always,* no matter how bad it is. They are almost certainly going to find out the truth anyway, and it's far better that they find it out from you than from someone else.

4. Own up to your mistakes. When you make a mistake, *own up to it.* Don't make excuses, and don't blame anybody else, even if you're not totally at fault. Take responsibility for what you've done. Say "I'm sorry," and mean it.

If your parents are like me, the one thing that will get you into *more* trouble when you mess up is lying about it and/or not taking responsibility for what you've done. When you make a mistake, often the first thing your parents want to know is whether you've learned from it.

"Repercussions" ("punishment" in my house) for various deeds and misdeeds are most likely doled out if your parents think you haven't learned from what you did—which means that you might do it again. Parents punish you to "help" you learn what not to do again.

Now, I know this is news to some of you, but your parents don't enjoy punishing you. No one enjoys watching someone they love suffer.

So if your parents can see that you're truly sorry for what you've done—and not just faking sorrow to impress them—they're less likely to punish you.

Taking responsibility means shouldering consequences. If you get punished, sulking won't get you anywhere. (In my house sulking kills any chance that I'll reduce the "sentence.") Sulking just says to your parents that you're not taking responsibility for what you've done and that you didn't learn from your mistake.

If you *have* lost your parents' trust, accept that fact (don't sulk about it) and work on rebuilding it. Trust can be rebuilt, but it takes time, prayer, and patience.

You've got to be willing to give your parents the time they need to rebuild trust in you. It'll happen, but you've got to be patient.

"WE ARGUE ALL THE TIME"

My parents and I get into arguments all the time. What can I do?

One of the things I tell my own children is that their mother and I are trying to prepare them for adulthood. And contrary to what you teenagers think, being an adult doesn't mean that no one ever tells you what to do anymore.

I'm an adult (an elected conference official), but I have someone down the hall from me (the conference president) who tells me *what to do*, occasionally *where to go*, and sometimes *where I can't go*. His demands aren't unreasonable *most* of the time (I'm going to show him this!), and he doesn't spend a lot of time breathing down my neck, telling me what to do. But when he *does* tell me to do something, he expects me to do it.

My point is, there will *always* be *somebody* in your life who will tell you what to do.

If you're a young person living at home, your parents are at the top of the list of people who tell you what to do, where to go, when to come in, etc. This is a fact of life— parents *can* tell you what to do, they *will* tell you what to do, and they *should* tell you what to do.

For some young people, half their problem with their parents is an unwillingness to accept that their parents will tell them what to do. Your parents have the right and responsibility to provide direction for your life. And as long as you're living with them, refusing to accept their direction will only place you in a fight you can't win.

Accepting this reality helps, and so does a belief and trust that your parents love you and really want what's best for you (*and* they usually know better than you what's best for you). No, your parents aren't perfect (you knew that already), nor are they always right. But they're right more often than you think.

If you have good parents (and most of you do), you can remove some of this parent/teenager strife by giving them the benefit of the doubt sometimes. Assume that they do love you and that they know what they're talking about.

"THEY TELL ME WHO TO DATE"

There's this guy in my church who likes me. My family keeps telling me that I should date him instead of the non-Adventist guy I'm dating. What do you think?

First, let me point out that dating outside the church goes contrary to the counsel in the Scriptures (see 2 Corinthians 6:14) and is, therefore, *wrong.* No one wants to say that, including me. But when *God* says don't do something, what else can *I* say?

But it intrigues me that your Adventist family is insisting that you date a particular Adventist guy. This is why I want to talk about the role I think parents should play in teenage dating.

My daughter, Courtney, won't have to worry about *me* insisting that she date anybody! I'm not going to hurry her into any relationship, at least not until she finishes grad school. (By *that* time I might do some "hurrying." Do you think I want her to live with me forever and spend my money forever? No way [smile]!)

Anyway, I'm not comfortable with parents "arranging" relationships. Parents aren't the ones who have to make the relationships work—their teenagers do.

So I may like someone for Courtney (and I *do* tend to like fellows she has no interest in at all). But I wouldn't be in the relationship with them—she would.

Arranging relationships for my daughter is not my role. My role as a parent is to help Courtney make it into God's kingdom.

Now, from what I've seen during my 21 years as a pastor and from what I've read in the Bible, I'm convinced that if Courtney were to date and marry a non-Adventist, that choice might very well hinder her salvation. And I'm unwilling to let her take that chance. That goes for my son, R.J., too.

I'm unwilling to risk my children's souls. That means I won't allow either of them to date a non-Seventh-day Adventist as long as they live in my house. That's my role as their parent.

Now, if after my children leave my house they choose to be unequally yoked, that's on them. And I shall love them no matter what.

But they'll have no doubt that I disapprove of the relationship, because God disapproves of it.

"THEY'RE GETTING A DIVORCE"

My parents are going through a rough time in their marriage, and it looks like they're going to get a divorce. The worst part is that they tell me I can't tell anyone right now, and I'm about to explode! What should I do?

i really wish I knew who wrote this question, because I feel bad for you. But someone handed me this question anonymously while I was at a youth event. The good thing is that God knows who you are, and He's there for you even if your world is falling apart.

First of all, you have to respect your parents' wishes and keep their problems confidential. They're your parents, and you need to do what they ask. Also, to betray their confidence and reveal their problems to others is a breach of trust. You would be devastated if your parents betrayed *your* trust, so don't do that to them.

But that still leaves you "ready to explode," and understandably so. As a pastor I've had to deal with divorce situations for 21 years. I can assure you that divorce is emotionally devastating. It's quite possible that with all the things your parents are dealing with right now, they haven't even thought about what you're dealing with.

Also, in all the years I've dealt with troubled marriages in the church, I've noticed an unfortunate tendency on at least one person's part to be more interested in covering up the problem (so no one will know) than in fixing it.

Minus the Lord directly fixing things Himself (which He *can* do—but remember, He doesn't force His ways on anyone), about the only hope I can offer is that all of you might benefit from some kind of professional counseling.

Naturally, your parents' situation is eating you up, and you do need to talk to *someone*. Tell your parents that. Tell them that you love them both, and that the breaking up of their marriage is breaking *you* up.

Tell them that you need help dealing with this situation, and ask them to allow you to talk to a counselor (maybe your pastor, your school counselor, or some *Christian* counselor who doesn't know them). Your request might even motivate your parents to get counseling too.

There's no shame in admitting that you need help; you just need to get help from the right place.

"THEY DON'T APPROVE OF MY GUY"

I'm an 18-year-old girl in a small town. Mine is the only Adventist family for at least 100 miles, and we live two hours away from the nearest Adventist church.

Well, I've fallen in love with my best friend's brother, who's a member of another denomination. I want to date him, but my parents don't approve of us starting a relationship, because he's not an Adventist. What do you say?

It can't be easy to be an Adventist teenager out there alone. Fellowship is important, and living so far way from other Adventist teens makes that difficult.

I'm honored that you want to know what I have to say about your situation. I really am. But it's way more important to know what God has to say. And He says, "Be ye not unequally yoked."

And, my friend, that's exactly what would happen if you started a relationship with this young man. I personally believe that the single most effective tool the devil uses to trap God's people is to put them in relationships with people in the "world." If *you* were the devil, wouldn't *you* try that one?

While I was in college I wanted to be a lawyer, so I majored in political science. In one class I read that if you're running for office, you should think how you would campaign against *yourself* if you were your opponent. That way you're ready for almost anything.

So what kinds of temptations would *you* throw at you if you were the devil? Wouldn't you at least *consider* sending some nice non-Adventist guy into a lonely Adventist girl's path? She's the only Adventist for scores of miles, and her church is hours away, so there's little opportunity for her to have an Adventist boyfriend.

Wouldn't that be an almost irresistible temptation for that girl? And wouldn't it encourage her to make small compromises for the sake of the relationship, and later, larger ones?

It's not as if the devil doesn't have a track record in the get-'em-through-becoming-unequally-yoked business. First Kings 11:1-5 says the devil lured Solomon into sin with foreign women. The first, according to *Prophets and Kings,* was Pharaoh's daughter, whom Solomon was able to convert. But that only led him to get involved with more foreign women, who eventually "unconverted" him.

Just as Satan "hooked up" Solomon back then, he still hooks up people today. Why would he stop using a trap that works? It worked on Solomon, the wisest man who ever lived. And don't get me started on how well it worked on Samson, the strongest man who ever lived.

Am I saying that your relationship is of Satan? No, but I'm prepared to say that it's probably not of God.

So what should you do, especially since it's almost impossible for you to have an Adventist boyfriend?

Well, I hate to be the one to point this out, but who says you *have* to have a boyfriend right now? I don't want to come across as insensitive, but people always use this argument to justify their actions—"There's nobody *in* the church to date, so therefore I can date *outside* the church."

But who says you *have* to date? It would be *nice* to date. But wouldn't it be *better* to do what God says and trust Him to provide a companion in His time?

You also wrote, "I want to date *him*." Didn't Samson say to his father about Delilah, "Get *her* for me. She's the right one for me" (Judges 14:3)? Samson never asked *God* if she was the right one.

Having romantic feelings toward someone isn't a bad thing by itself. But it *is* if you want that person so badly that it doesn't matter to you whether or not God wants him/her for you.

You said that your parents don't approve of this relationship. Be *very* concerned about any relationship that your parents don't approve of.

This is particularly true if you live with both your parents. Usually one parent is more lenient about dating relationships than the other. (Guess who's the difficult parent in *my* house?) So if *both* your parents disapprove of the relationship, it's almost certainly a bad idea.

Even if you live with only one parent, listen to their counsel. Down deep almost every last one of you know that your parents are on your side. And they'll be there for you long after your boyfriend or girlfriend is gone.

Basically, we've just talked about what you *shouldn't* do. What *should* you do?

First, determine that all your relationships will meet God's approval.

Second, take advantage of all the opportunities your local church, conference, etc., provide for fellowship. Who knows? You might meet someone *there*.

Third, where you go to college is critical. If there are few Adventist young men in your church, why would you turn around and go to a non-Adventist college, where there are even *fewer*?

I know that I've been saying some tough-to-deal-with stuff. But I'll guarantee that it's not as tough to deal with as falling into the devil's trap and being lost.

Oh, I know a bunch of you are screaming, "How do you know that this relationship is the devil's trap?"

I don't know, at least not for sure. But I think it is. I mean, it's not as though the devil hasn't used this trap about a zillion times before.

Now I've got a question for you: how do you know that it's *not* a trap from the devil? Too many times we try to see how close we can come to the devil's ground without actually going there, when we *ought* to be staying as far away as we can.

You can play Russian roulette and dodge the bullet for a long time. But if you don't escape just once, you're dead. Then all the times you got away really don't matter. Don't play Russian roulette with your soul—please.

Make no mistake about it—for a lot of people, choosing whether or not to be unequally yoked is an eternal life-or-death decision.

"THEY TRY TO RUN MY LIFE"

It seems like my parents are always trying to run my life. Why can't they just let me make my own decisions?

In dealing with your parents, remember that there are a few basic rules. The sooner you follow these, the happier your teenage years will be.

1. Remember, your parents have the right and responsibility to provide at least some guidance for your life. I know some of you have this attitude: "It's my life." And that means no one is supposed to tell you what to do.

Hel-lo! This is your wake-up call. Everybody has somebody who tells them what to do at least some of the time.

We hire young people in my office every summer. One year a sweet young lady came to work for me partly, she said, so she could get away from home and live on her own. No one telling her what to do, right?

Not exactly. I told her what time to come to work and what time she could leave. Every day I told her what to do and how much time she had to get it done. We have a dress code in my office, which I enforced.

Her mother (the one she was trying to get away from for a while) *never* told her what she could and could not wear. I, on the other hand, was very specific about what I would and would not accept—which excluded half her wardrobe! She got more directions from me than she would have rebelled against at home.

But she never complained. It's called "growing up."

2. Trust your parents (especially since you want them to trust you). Believe that they really want what's best for you.

Do you really think that the same people who love you, who willingly make all kinds of sacrifices to make you happy, would then intentionally and arbitrarily make decisions that are designed to make you *unhappy?* Does that make *sense?*

3. Know the "nonnegotiables"—the areas in which your parents are not likely to back down. For me, those are such things as obedience, respect, modesty in dress, attendance in church school, etc. In my house it does no good for my children to argue about those things. I've told my daughter, "You might think Daddy's crazy, but he's not going to change."

There's no point in fighting over the nonnegotiables, so respect your parents' wishes in those areas and try to negotiate compromise in other areas.

For example, I'm a firm believer in Christian education. I'm not sending my children to any school that's not Seventh-day Adventist. That's a nonnegotiable.

On the other hand, I'm a little more flexible on things such as, oh, say, my son's hairstyle. He had an Afro last fall—I didn't like it. But I compromised and told him that as long as he kept it neatly combed, he could have it.

Most parents are willing to compromise except in areas of principle and "Thus saith the Lord." Now, you might not agree with what your parents think is a principle or a "Thus saith the Lord." That's not the point.

Sometimes my daughter pulls out her "But Daddy, that's not fair!" I tell her (jokingly), "I'm the daddy; I don't have to be fair."

What I *really* mean by that is—I am not bound by her definition of what's fair. Someone has to set the rules, and in our house there is a name for those people. They're called *parents.*

4. Remember, trust has to be earned. You have to prove to your parents that you're responsible and trustworthy enough for them to "let go" of you—at least a little. Face it, most of the things you want to do (driving, dating, going out with your friends) involve some risk.

Why would you expect that the people who love you more than anything, who have spent their entire lives protecting you from risk, and whose worst nightmare is that something will happen to you, would now unhesitatingly allow you to do things that potentially carry big risks?

Put yourself in your parents' place, and then demonstrate that you will conduct yourself in a way that minimizes those risks.

5. Finally, when you do get in an argument, be respectful. Telling your parents off may feel good in the short run, but you'll feel bad later. And you'll drive a wedge between you and the people who love you more than *anything* and who will be there for you longer than *anybody.*

9

Friends and Peers

"MY FRIEND BUGS ME"

I have this friend who really bugs me because she focuses on herself. She always borrows my clothes, but never gives them back. I want to do the right thing, but I'm getting tired of the way she acts. Please help!

Every friendship involves trade-offs. Since no friend (except Jesus) is perfect, we all put up with our friends' bad points because we like their good points. And don't forget, *your* friends put up with you the same way!

In a relationship each of us has to decide if the good outweighs the bad, and whether the friendship is worth what it takes to maintain it. I'll say this: *true* friendship is pretty rare, and it's usually worth putting up with a few things to maintain it.

On the other hand, some problems are preventable. For instance, unless your friend is putting a gun to your head when she asks to borrow your clothes, you can say no. You can also tell her *why* you're saying no—because she doesn't bring your clothes *back*. Tell her that this is coming between your friendship.

Now, *how* you say all these things is *very* important. If the next time your friend comes to borrow a dress you attack her as if it's judgment day—well, that's not going to do it. But if you tell her about your feelings calmly, carefully, and prayerfully, that will help.

Well, she might get mad *anyway,* and you might lose her as a friend. But if you *don't* talk this over with her, *you'll* be so mad at her that you'll end up losing her friendship anyway.

If you think about it, you probably became friends in the first place because you enjoyed talking to each other. So try talking now, and if it doesn't work, just remember that a relationship in which two people can't talk things over will eventually bite the dust.

Don't talk *about* her—as a lot of people would do. Talk *to* her instead.

"THEY'RE SPREADING LIES ABOUT ME"

Two sisters in my class tell lies about me to my classmates and right to my face. When I tell my parents what these girls are doing, they talk to the principal, and then he talks to the girls. But they deny everything, and I look silly.

Because of what's going on I'm upset a lot of the time, and I dread going to school. This is even affecting my health. What should I do?

It's certainly no fun to be picked on. When I was young, people used to say, "Sticks and stones may break my bones, but words can never hurt me."

What a false statement! I've never had any bones broken by sticks or stones, but I've been hurt by people's words plenty of times.

Every school seems to have a bully, who physically or verbally terrorizes other students. I used to tell my children that I'd punish them big-time if I ever found out they were doing anything like that. In particular, I told them they'd be toast if I found out they were talking negatively about anyone's looks, intellect, or family economic position.

The problem with verbal bullies is that they'll say anything about anyone. Sometimes they zero in on a target or two and act as if their aim in life is to make that person (or persons) miserable. Worse yet, these "verbal terrorists" often scare everyone else away from their victim(s). So people are afraid that if they speak up for the one(s) being picked on, they'll be next.

So what do you do? First, it's not a good idea to get down on these girls' level by being as mean and ugly to them as they've been to you. Aside from the fact that it's un-Christlike, it probably won't do you any good anyway.

Verbal bullies are usually very gifted in expressing themselves. So by the time you deliver that witty comeback it took you weeks to come up with, they'll have launched four or five "verbal missiles" back at you. They'll blow your one little comeback out of the water and make you look really bad. Face it, they're better at that kind of thing than you are.

So don't try to "out-diss" verbal bullies. You can't beat them at what they do best, especially if they operate without rules.

What I mean is that they'll say *anything* about you. But because you're not like that, you won't talk about them the way they'll talk about you. It would be like trying to beat Michael Jordan playing one-on-one on his home court, while you had to follow the rules of basketball and he didn't. You'd get slaughtered. (Of course, if you tried to play basketball with Michael Jordan, you'd get slaughtered anyway.)

Well, what can you do? There's no easy way to deal

with this issue—I wish there were. But you can handle it in one of two ways.

First, you can handle it yourself, which is the best way—if you can. The second way is to ask some key adults to help you, which you've already done. (I'll talk about that later.)

Handling this situation yourself doesn't mean you should "get down on their level" and act as ugly toward these girls as they've acted toward you.

As I've pointed out, first of all, it's *wrong*. Can you *imagine* Jesus doing that? And second, it's a bad idea because these girls have already demonstrated that no one can handle them when it comes to ugly words.

Remember that dealing with this problem in the right way won't achieve instant results, though. You've got to stick with it for the long haul.

Now, here's my advice. First, you've got to discipline yourself not to show any anger—*at all, ever*—when the verbal abuse starts. If you don't get upset, you make yourself a considerably less-attractive target.

Second, figure out a way to respond to these sisters that's kind but firm. Try taking the offensive. Instead of waiting for one of the verbal bullies to "attack" you, speak first. Say, "What's up, Sue?" And when she goes on the attack, say, "I don't like what you're saying about me, but we're still cool."

Third, when one or both of them attack someone else in your presence, defend the person who's being attacked. Try to end the attack by saying, "Leave them alone, Sue; they aren't doing anything to you."

Stick up for others, but be prepared—the sisters will probably turn their attack back on you. Often one or two verbally-aggressive people dominate a whole group—but only if the group *allows* it.

Finally, though young people don't always want to do it this way, some things are best handled adult to adult. If what I've suggested doesn't work, maybe you could have a conference with both sets of parents and the principal.

If you think the principal or the girls' parents aren't inclined to believe you, bring a witness along. Surely someone's seen what's going on.

There *is* a way to keep these girls from making your life miserable. Now ask the Lord to help you find it.

"WHY ARE THEY STUCK-UP?"

Why are Seventh-day Adventist academy kids so stuck-up?

First of all, that sounds like a generalization to me. There are scores of academies in North America that literally tens of thousands of students attend, and I don't believe that *all* of those students are stuck-up. Neither do I think that you really believe that.

It's true that *some* academy kids *are* stuck-up, but so are some kids who *don't* attend Adventist academies. What I think is more likely happening is that you're seeing people with a lot of things in common hang out together. This is natural, and sometimes it happens unintentionally.

I don't think the students mean to exclude other people around them. It's just that natural bonds do form among people who have the same friends and the same teachers, and complain about the same cafeteria food (at least boarding school students do). All these things unite academy students together so tightly that if you're *not* attending their school, you could feel left out.

So what can you do about it? First, remember that while you don't have to like someone's behavior or agree with it, it always helps to understand why people act the way they do. As we already pointed out, people with common experiences tend to bond with one another.

Now, I have *very* mixed feelings about my academy years. The academy I attended was about 90 percent White, and this was back in the 1970s. At that time my school wasn't exactly racially sensitive or racially progressive. So academy wasn't always a happy place for me.

But I did get excited when I went back for my class reunion. I was even glad to see people there that I hadn't particularly enjoyed seeing when we were students. We were, and always will be, bound by a common experience—attending the same school.

For you the trick is to find common ground with the academy students and build relationships with them when you don't have an academy experience in common—or any other common thread.

Now, if it was easy to find common ground, people would do it more often. But there are some things that you *can* do to build bridges.

If you're in academy or a part of whatever group happens to be "the group," try to reach out to those on the "outside," particularly if the outsiders have no control over the reason they're outside.

And don't say "But we have nothing in common!" Until you make an effort to get to know someone, how do you know what you have in common? Most of you are missing out on the opportunity to get to know some great people because you won't venture outside your "group."

We as humans tend to prejudge people or groups with whom we have little contact or of whom we have little knowledge. So people end up saying such things as "Academy kids are stuck-up" or "Black people are this way" or "White people are this way," when the truth is that once you really get to know people who are not like you or not in your group, you find out that "they" are a lot more like "you" than you thought. Give them a chance.

Also, do *something* with someone with whom you ordinarily do nothing. Invite them to your house, your church, or the mall. Make sure that when your "group" is around people who aren't in "the group," you include everyone in the conversation.

If you're not in "the group," it's a little harder. But you still have to reach out. You can do some inviting too. It's risky—you could get embarrassed. But no relationship is without risk. A greater risk is to go through life poorer because you know only people who are like you.

If you talk *to* people who are not like you—instead of talking *about* them—in many cases you'll find that you'll have more friends and a richer life.

"MY FRIEND'S PREGNANT"

I have a friend who's pregnant and too young to handle the responsibility. She came to me for moral support. What do I say?

There's no magic answer to your question. I can only imagine the emotions that are going through your friend's mind—fear, guilt, and shame for letting her family and friends down. I would think that the situation could seem overwhelming to her.

Young ladies, if you're thinking about becoming sexually active, or if you are sexually active, you're most likely headed toward unplanned, unwed, early motherhood. And I'll say this: when it happens to you, you won't like it.

Now let me back up and answer the question about your pregnant friend. I've been in your shoes before. In particular, I remember warning a young person (whom I kind of adopted) that she was going to get burned if she kept playing with fire.

Sadly, she did get pregnant. But when that happened, I assured her that nothing had changed between us.

I think this is what your friend needs to hear right now—that you are still her friend even though she's pregnant. That you accept her even though she's done something you consider unacceptable.

I told my friend to call me if she needed anything. And then, just as I'd done before, I called her periodically to let her know that I was concerned about her.

When her baby was born, I went to see her and told her that just as I had adopted her, I was now adopting her baby. And I did.

Try to get the message across to your friend that while this pregnancy will complicate her life immensely, she can still make something of herself with the Lord's help. And assure her that you'll be there to help too.

"I LIKE SOMEONE MY FRIEND LIKES"

Should your friends be mad at you if you go out with someone they like?

The short answer is no, they shouldn't be mad at you. In fact, they should be happy because you're happy. But the reality is your friends *do* get mad sometimes.

Now, you can handle that reality in one of two ways. You can get mad at your friends for being so insecure and selfish that they can't be happy for you. Or you can remember that if you have real friends, they'll be around for you long after you've forgotten about your boyfriend/girlfriend.

I know that sometimes friends can be a real pain. But remember, they're friends, not angels. And part of the deal of friendship is being friends with people *because of* and *despite* who they are. Your friends must do that for you too.

Instead of getting mad, try to understand how your friend is feeling. You and your friend liked the same person. You got the person, and your friend didn't. That's a *little* hard to take, especially if you end up with a boyfriend/girlfriend and your friend winds up alone.

Then, because you have a boyfriend/girlfriend, now your friends end up spending less time with you, so they lose again! Plus, they probably feel guilty for not being happy for you.

If you and your friends are patient and honest with each other, you can get through this. Pay attention to how your friends handle this; almost inevitably, one day you'll find yourself in the same situation.

"WHAT IF MY FRIEND'S DRINKING OR ON DRUGS?"

How can I tell if a friend is drinking or on drugs? What's the best way to approach them to get them to talk to me about it so I can help?

I'm not sure there's one "best" approach. But since my wife works at a center for people battling substance abuse, I asked her your questions. (That's supposed to make you think, *He does his homework!* Actually, it's to get you to blame *her* and not me if you disagree with what's coming next!)

My wife and her colleagues at the Alcohol and Drug Council of Middle Tennessee have identified classic signs of alcohol or drug abuse. You might want to see if any of the following behaviors fit your friend:

1. Constantly talks about using alcohol or drugs.
2. Has unusual temper outbursts or unusual depression.

147

3. Abruptly changes behavior, such as school performance. (Falling grades should be a major warning sign. People who've been getting A's all their lives don't suddenly just start getting D's without a reason. And the reason is always something bad.)

4. Starts acting irrational and paranoid.

5. Gets in trouble with the law.

6. Gets suspended from school for a drug-related incident. (I know this one sounds obvious, but it isn't always. Often when people get caught, they try to explain everything away with such excuses as "This was my first time" or "I was carrying drugs for someone else," etc. Be very skeptical about those claims.)

7. Makes frequent, secretive trips to the closet or the bathroom (to use drugs).

8. Steals items from home or employer.

9. Associates with known drug dealers.

10. Lets physical appearance and grooming habits deteriorate.

11. Constantly wears sunglasses.

Now, people may exhibit these traits without being into drugs and/or alcohol. For example, some of you think it's cool to wear sunglasses at night, even when there's no sun. (Remember, though, that they're called *sun*glasses!")

But if your friend is exhibiting several of these signs *together,* then he or she probably has a problem with drugs or alcohol.

If this is the case, there are some things you *shouldn't* do for your friend. (Again, special thanks to my wife and her colleagues for this information.)

In order to help your friend:

1. *Don't* cover up, make excuses, or take on your friend's responsibilities. This is almost invariably what family members and friends do at first because they think they're helping—or at least protecting the family name. In

reality, they might as well be giving the person the alcohol or drugs. They're "enabling" the abuse, and are thus known as "enablers." (And as a pastor, I've met them.)

2. *Don't* nag or lecture your friend.

3. *Don't* have the misunderstanding that overcoming dependency is just a matter of willpower.

4. *Don't* threaten your friend about his or her abuse. If you say something, say what you mean and mean what you say. And always follow through on your word.

5. *Don't* let your friend persuade you to join him or her in the use of alcohol or drugs. Your friend might try to tell you that if you join in, he or she will do it less. But that won't happen. If you condone the habit by joining in, you'll just make your friend feel less of a need to get help.

6. *Don't* forget that *no one*—not even your friend—is beyond the power of God. He can and will help anyone who wants His help, and allows Him to come in and take over the problem.

That brings us to what you *should* do for a friend who's using alcohol or drugs.

The first place to go for help is obviously God. Addiction can be such a deep-rooted emotional and psychological problem that it requires a lot of help. That's because the devil *never* tells you when he gets you *into* something that he has no intention of letting you *out* of it. And "recovery" for many addicts is a continuing process. Often people with addiction problems refer to themselves as "recovering alcoholics or addicts," even if they haven't touched alcohol or drugs in years.

God is stronger than the devil and addiction, though. And He not only helps us Himself—He has people on earth trained to help. I'm grateful to Elvina Wolcott, from Adventist PlusLine, for providing the following list of places you and your friend can contact for help.

I haven't dealt with any of these organizations personally, so I can't tell you a whole lot about them. But the fact that this list comes from Adventist PlusLine makes me feel comfortable about passing it on to you.

But remember, if your friend won't seek help, there's not much you can do. But there's nothing *God* can't do. So sometimes the only thing you can do is to turn the situation over to God. Of course, that's a pretty good place to leave problems anyway.

ADDICTION RESOURCES

Organization/Address	Telephone/Fax/E-mail
The Bridge Fellowship*	(502) 777-1094
Carol and Paul Cannon	(502) 777-1062 (fax)
1745 Logsdon Road	
Bowling Green, KY 42101	
www.bridgefellowship.org	
Drug Alternative Program (DAP)*	
11868 Arliss Dr.	
Grand Terrace, CA 92324	
Insight Treatment Program	(626) 564-2703
Anthony Lopez, Director	(818) 990-4603 (fax)
1155 East Green Street	
Pasadena, CA 91106	
Loma Linda University*	1-800-752-5999
Behavioral Medicine Center	(909) 335-4262 (fax)
710 Barton Rd.	
Redlands, CA 92373	
New Life Treatment Centers, Inc.	1-800-NEW-LIFE
	webmaster@newlife.com

Tennessee Christian Medical Center*   (615) 865-2373
500 Hospital Drive   (615) 865-0251
Madison, TN 37115   (615) 860-6311 (fax)

---

*Denotes an Adventist-affiliated institution.

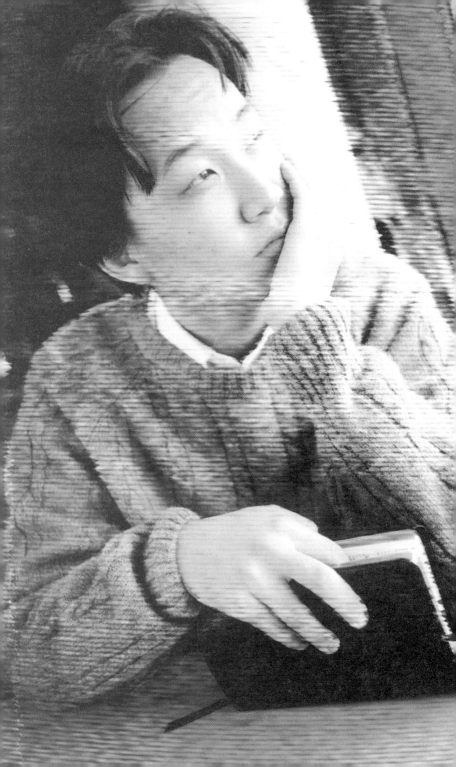

10

Me, Myself, and I

"I'M REALLY DEPRESSED"

I read about Kyla Marden's struggle with depression in the September 19, 1998, issue of *Insight,* and I'm going through the same thing. What can I do? I feel like I'm in a deep hole, and I don't see a way out.

i'm no authority on depression and its cure, but here are some things to consider. First, it's important for you to know that you aren't the only one struggling with depression.

Sometimes when we have a problem, we feel weird or strange because of it. But lots of people struggle with depression, and it's nothing to be ashamed of.

Depression is an illness (at least I believe it is), and you ought not to be ashamed that you have this particular illness any more than you should be ashamed of having the flu. It's what you do about your depression that counts.

I do believe that some people are more naturally inclined to be depressed because they have a more melancholic nature, just as it's natural for some people to be taller or shorter or lighter or darker. Depression is something some people have to deal with, while others don't.

I don't point out these things to minimize your problem. I just want to help those of you struggling with depression to understand it a little better.

Depression *is* a problem, but it's not an unbeatable problem. And you're not abnormal or weird if you struggle with it. Actually, everybody has problems—that's normal. It's just that depression is a problem that's a little more difficult to handle sometimes.

Where can you go to get help? This may sound weird, but you might want to start by seeing a physician. *Some* depression is rooted in physical (not emotional) problems. Consider these questions: Are you eating a balanced diet? Are you getting enough sleep? Depending on your answers, a doctor may or may not refer you to a psychologist for treatment and/or medication.

Depression is quite often curable, but it's easier to cure when we understand what's causing it.

There are some organizations run by our church that may be able to help too. I haven't dealt with any of them personally, but I'm comfortable recommending them because I found out about them from Adventist PlusLine, an organization run by our church.

The names of these organizations are: the New Life Clinic in Plano, Texas (phone: 1-800-639-5433) and the Rapha Hospital Treatment Center in Atlanta, Georgia (1-800-383-HOPE). That last phone number, which spells "hope," is really significant because depression often makes people feel hopeless.

But there's *always* hope—as long as you're alive. In the September 19 issue of *Insight* that you referred to, Kyla talked about her battle with depression and about how she *won* that battle. Depression *is* curable. If Kyla can overcome it, so can you!

Building a friendship with God, I believe, is the most

important step to getting well. In *addition* to everything else we've mentioned, you're going to have to ask the Lord at the *beginning* of *every* day to help you change your thoughts.

The devil's the one who puts depressing, negative thoughts in our minds. And we've got to ask the Lord to help us not to believe that liar!

Every time the devil tries to make you think you aren't a valuable person (you *are,* especially to God!), remind him that *he's* the worthless one. One day you'll be the one sitting with Jesus at His welcome table—and the devil will be toast!

"I DON'T LIKE MYSELF SOMETIMES"

I get depressed, and I don't like myself sometimes. What can I do?

As crazy as it might sound, I think consistent exercise is an important way to combat depression.

I just lost 25 pounds through a diet plan combined with working out three days a week. And speaking from experience, I can tell you that exercise made me feel better physically. Plus it gave me a sense of accomplishment, which helped me feel better about myself.

I believe that exercise can do these same things for you. After all, not feeling good about yourself is a big part of what depression is all about.

Exercise also helps you get off the I-don't-like-how-I-look-so-I-get-depressed-and-eat-which-makes-me-gain-weight-which-makes-me-depressed-which-makes-me-eat-which-makes-me-gain-weight-which-makes-me-depressed, etc., etc., merry-go-round.

Regular vigorous exercise is likely to have a positive

effect on your weight. And it will slow down your trips to the dinner table! Why? Because you won't want to go back to the way you used to be.

I'll admit that starting and sticking to an exercise plan is tough, especially at first. When I began exercising, my body said things to me like "What *is* this new thing [exercise] that you're doing to me?"

But now that I've worked so hard to get in shape, I don't want to eat the way I used to.

Besides exercising, I recommend that you find something to do—something you're good at that interests you. If you don't start a hobby or two, you'll have too much time to focus on what's wrong with you. And you might forget that *everybody* has *something* about themselves they wish they could change.

Also, don't fail to find and do something for somebody else *daily*. You're *always* going to be able to find people who are worse off than you are. By helping *them,* you'll help *yourself,* because it'll make you feel good! Helping others will always turn your negative thoughts about yourself into positive ones.

WHERE'S ELDER EDMOND?

You can find Elder Edmond in the pages of *Insight* magazine every week, where he's busy solving your problems. To make sure you get *Insight* at your church, see your youth leader or church Sabbath school secretary.

www.insightmagazine.org
1-800-765-6955